BICYCLE TOURING
Utah

BICYCLE TOURING
Utah

DENNIS COELLO
Maps by DAVID TAFF

 Northland Press

For Wally

Other books by Dennis Coello

Bicycle Touring Arizona (Northland Press)
Bicycle Touring Colorado (in progress, Northland Press)
Living on Two Wheels (Ross Books)
Mountain Bike Manual (Dream Garden Press)
Mountain Bike Rides of the West (Northland Press)
Roadside Guide to Bike Repairs (Ross Books; second edition Warner Books)
Touring on Two Wheels (Nick Lyons Books)
The Trailside Guide (Nick Lyons Books)

CONTENTS

PREFACE

I grew up in St. Louis, where the Missouri flows into the Big Muddy. In 1985, on my first long bike tour, I followed the Mississippi north to the Great Lakes, circled Superior, then pedalled along countless Midwest streams on my way home. In the Army I spent time on the Mekong. Later, on my round-the-world ride in 1974, I followed rivers through twenty countries, and marvelled at the blue oceans which would finally appear.

There was always water. Thus the shock of desert scrub and slickrock was great when I moved to Utah from a greener world. I was unprepared for cities not built along rivers, ignorant of snowpacks and cactus, diamondbacks and salt flats.

Nor had I ever seen a land of such drastic contrasts. In all my riding I'd never begun a day with a hot forty-mile, desert run, then spent an hour climbing into aspen and evergreen, just to endure a hailstorm while hidden beneath a juniper, before ending the ride in a cold mountain rain. It was obvious I had a lot to learn about biking in Utah.

The knowledge has come slowly—through seven years of one- and two-week rides, year-round commuting, weekend exploration tours, and, finally, thirty-five hundred miles in a single summer.

So what have I learned? All that I need to stay alive, of course; the best roads with the least traffic; which towns are nonexistent (though still on the map); where to enjoy a great meal and a good motel; campgrounds and waterholes and what to carry with me in all seasons. But beyond remaining alive has come appreciation of the different landforms and animals, why some plants make it in the desert and some don't, of all the natural history which bikers, especially, have the time to get to know.

Non-bikers often ask why a car isn't preferable for travel—especially in a state of such great distances. Their question arises from the misconception that viewing the landscape through a windshield is the same as looking at it over the handlebars. But the two forms of travel are inherently different. One presents a scene for casual observation; the other involves the observer as active participant, demanding his attention to temperature, topography, possible weather changes, wind speed and direction, tumbleweeds, et cetera.

Thus cyclists experience the land as fully as those who first traversed it, and are linked to them by shared concerns and common ordeal. Especially in Utah, where deserts and mountain ranges make travel difficult, and civilization exists only in isolated cities and towns, the biker can quickly feel at one with those who went before. Centuries-old diary entries about the heat and wind and alkali, penned by travelers at the mercy of the elements, are easily understood by today's cyclists. No other form of modern travel allows such a sharing of history.

But the beauty is also shared—the grandeur of a 360° view from the saddle (be it on a horse or bike) of the state's five national parks, two huge national recreation areas, and six national monuments. Pedal the sage-covered countryside as an orange sun sets behind a mountain, smell the air as it cools in evening and the deer begin to feed, and you'll never again question the difference between driving and biking in Utah.

And then there are the people. More than with any other mode of travel, a biker learns a state through the folks who fill his water bottles, let him sleep in their fields, and answer his questions about the road ahead.

I didn't know much of the history of Utah before pedalling it, traversing the same trails as Bridger and Beckwourth, Dominguez and Escalante. Like so many outsiders, I thought all Utah history was "church" history, and assumed I was leaving the immigrant story when I left St. Louis. I did not expect to find a state of such historical richness—from Indian ruins built in Caesar's day and Spanish trails two hundred years old, to mountain men and Mormons and a series of settlements whose names display their origins—Jap Town, Greek Town, Little Italy, and more. There are Basque sheepherders here who still speak little English, Chinese whose ancestors helped drive the Golden Spike, Japanese who in 1900 set up a sugar beet factory in Delta, and forty years later were held prisoner in the nearby Topaz Internment Camp.

I've ridden past the place where a hundred emigrants were slaughtered by the Mormons, and pedalled into nearby towns to ask why. The stories came, of Haun's Mill and Carthage, of Winter Quarters and the Mormon War. I've cycled by the waters which sped the one-armed surveyor John Wesley Powell to fame, journeyed the same roads as the Hole-in-the-Rock company, pedalled the Salt Flats and stared at Pilot Peak, recalling the Donner Party who black-tongued their way across and resorted to desperate means to stay alive that winter.

This book is a guide to the past and a knowledgeable present, through the slow cycling of today's trails. For a weekend ride or month-long tour, there's no better way to experience Utah.

A NOTE ON ORGANIZATION

As you can see from the chapter maps, I've divided the state into eight major loops. Each loop has one or more "spurs" coming from it. Loops are numbered, spurs are assigned letters. In this manner one of your group can suggest: "How about doing spur D of Loop 2 this weekend?"; the friend on the phone can quickly refer to the Table of Contents to find the correct page, read the entry, and decide against it when he sees there isn't a Holiday Inn in Mexican Hat.

At the beginning of each chapter (one chapter for each loop) I'll provide an overall sketch of the loop's terrain, history, natural features, and if critical, distances between water. Some of the longer historical trails will be encountered on several loops; I'll discuss them at length in one chapter, and merely refer to that passage in the rest. I'll also list the length for the loop and each spur, and suggest which season is best for travel.

However, I won't be so detailed as to ruin your sense of discovery. The biker has chosen *the* mode of travel *most* affected by the elements. Such a personality would chafe against a guide which told of every hill.

After the loops comes a chapter on shorter rides, especially ones originating along the Wasatch Front. I've tried to develop these weekend jaunts into tiny loops, to avoid the "out and back" problem of cycling in areas which lack a thorough secondary road network. Of course, all the loops and spurs can themselves be broken up into shorter rides. For this reason, and because I include other information in earlier loops which will be useful in later ones, this short guide will serve best when read in its entirety.

Next, I'll escort you along the only major out-of-state run in the book—the ride to Yellowstone. The Park's narrow roads turn cars into more frightful beasts than grizzlies, but there are ways to handle that problem. And the ride up! It was my first real taste of the alpine West, and there's no prettier range than the Tetons.

I've provided an equipment list, though if you've toured before you no doubt have your own. Each item's purpose is described in my first book, *Living on Two Wheels*, and if I may make one suggestion to even the veteran cyclists among us—don't underestimate this state. Its blue skies and sweet sage will lull you into carelessness, and then a squall will hit. I've shoulder-packed my bike through snow on summer days, and baked an hour later after a ten mile descent. Fail to saddlebag the essentials and you stand a chance to become one with the alkali.

A word on mileages. I have to assume most of us don't ride with odometers, and therefore must communicate distances through other reference points. Mileposts—those green rectangular signs most noticeable on Kansas turnpikes—are great for bikers. I'll abbreviate them as **MP**. But some roads aren't graced with these green signs, and in such cases I'll fall back on that which one can read in the diaries of explorers and pioneers— "halfway up the mountainside, where juniper turns to evergreen," or "just go till you smell water."

The Utah Travel Council has two publications that might be of interest. The first is the *Utah Travel Guide*. Its primary value to bikers lies in its listing of the hundreds of camping sites in the state, and the names, addresses, phone numbers, and prices of hotels and motels in each town. Updated each year, the *Guide* is available free of charge from:

Utah Travel Council
Council Hall, Capitol Hill
300 N. State Street
Salt Lake City, Utah 84114
801-533-5681

Residents of Salt Lake Valley are requested to pick up the booklet at the Utah Travel Council office; those who live elsewhere need only write or call for a copy to be mailed to them—again at no charge.

The second publication is the Multipurpose Map Series—five (formerly eight) detailed topographic maps. (At the time of this printing the Travel Council had not decided upon the cost; call or write for this information. The maps are expected to be available to the public as of July 1987.) I highly recommend that you pack along the appropriate one for the loop you will be traveling, as they contain detailed information impossible to include in the general maps in this book. If you do not have one of these maps, you should at least carry a Utah highway map—available at many locations throughout the state—to augment the small, less detailed maps in this book.

The restrictions of size and weight—so critical to cyclists—have kept this book quite small. So don't get your feelings hurt if I've shortchanged your favorite area, or failed to mention your home town. If you really want it included drop me a line, and make your friends buy the book. Maybe then it will appear in a second edition.

The author would like to acknowledge the prompt and thorough replies received concerning specific regulations and advice for cyclists in the following National Park Service areas: Larry E. Florea, Zion National Park; Joan M. Anzelmo, Yellowstone National Park; Jon M. James, Golden Spike National Historic Site; John T. Conoboy, Cedar Breaks National Monument; Ed Christian, Grand Teton National Park; Eleanor Inskip, Canyonlands/Arches National History Association; Thomas E. Henry, Bryce Canyon National Park.

INTRODUCTION—
GETTING STARTED

This chapter is included primarily for those who have never toured by bike. Perhaps you've wanted to, but judged your physical condition too poor for the road, or were filled with fears of mechanical breakdowns. Maybe the questions of what to pack, how to carry it, and where to stay at night have plagued you to inaction. Or you may have never had the slightest desire to tour on two wheels, and are reading this book merely for one-day outings.

Well, give it a chance. In my first book, *Living on Two Wheels*, I dealt with all those nagging problems inherent in preparing for one's first tour. My next book, *Roadside Guide to Bike Repairs*, is a slim volume designed for the non-mechanic cyclist. Let me pull from them a few points which might be appropriate here, and try to dispel doubts which remain about touring. Review the other books for more thorough information, or talk with riders who've been on the road before. While it's true that experience is the best teacher, it doesn't have to be *your* hard-earned experience.

I wrote in *Living* that touring by bicycle is, for me, "the quintessential element in satisfying the age-old urge of mankind: discovery." A well-tuned bike makes possible easy movement across miles of different kinds of terrain—allowing the experience and "feel" of geographically diverse regions in a manner unknown to faster travellers. Cyclists also come to know the people along their routes, when asking for water, directions, or permission to camp nearby. Perhaps it's the simple, unobtrusive mode of travel which puts people so at ease; in over two decades and hundreds of requests I've seldom been turned down.

Beyond the places and people, cycling allows—and often demands—a constant succession of other discoveries. The smell of rain in the air minutes before a storm; head winds; severe temperature changes; the differences in flowers, animals, and insects of various regions; knowledge of them all comes to the touring cyclist who rides with senses open and alert.

Drive the state of Utah and view its rugged beauty and vast expanses. Pedal it, and become part of its deserts and mountains—subject to the same forces which created the land. That thought should intrigue, not frighten. With careful preparation one can handle everything one finds on and off the road.

Before preparing for a ride, you'll have to determine which kind of tour you'll be taking. You can plan a trip in which you'll stay indoors each night, thereby eliminating the weight of tent and sleeping bag. You might choose a route with nightly motel stops every 35 to 50 miles—a pleasurable daily distance—especially with a minimum of gear. Or you might choose to camp, with daily rides of 80 to 100 miles. While we're on the topic of where to sleep, let me warn you against campgrounds when they're busy. Avoid these noisy nylon subdivisions, and instead request permission from farmers, ranchers, homeowners, churches, or small town sheriffs to throw up your tent in their domain. The resulting conversations often lead to shared meals, long interesting evenings and indelible memories.

In *Living* a twelve-week training program is detailed for those with little cycling experience, who are in minimal physical condition, and who wish to be able to tour 35 to 50 mpd (miles per day) with full equipment. For more than two decades I've used this regimen to prepare people of all ages for the road—and had problems only when someone failed to train as suggested.

Herculean strength is unnecessary; endurance is the key. Begin with very short rides over level ground on a stripped bike and gradually work up from there. Everything will be sore at first—contact points (especially one's bottom), and muscle groups in the arms, shoulders, neck, trunk, and legs. If you think cycling only builds legs, try it. Pump a loaded bike over hills for a few hours when you're not in shape, and you'll know the next day *exactly* how many muscles are involved. But build to that point slowly, adding weight as strength and handling ability increase, and thereby avoid the pain.

My favorite kind of cycle tour—and one which I strongly suggest for Utah riding—is the combination motel/camping tour. While this does require you to carry considerably more weight than a motel trip, it frees you from the necessity of riding every day to a pre-determined point, and of fear of not making it there. Through avoidance of schedules, and of the work-a-day world's constant "disciplined time," a tour becomes a true vacation.

Use this book to determine your route, supplement it with multipurpose maps and a hotel/motel guide, and then enter into this equation your available money and time. If the itinerary requires that you forego that extra hour with a newspaper at breakfast, or rush away from chance conversations, choose a shorter ride. Unlike backpacking, after cycle touring you'll remember *people* as well as places. (Furthermore, you won't feel like a mule with weight on your shoulders, or be reminded of forced marches in the service.)

The next consideration in planning a tour should be traveling companions. I prefer solo riding, for reasons which will become clear when you read the following chapters. Friends have asked if I'm unconcerned about the possibility of becoming sick or hurt so far from home—between towns perhaps—and all alone. My reply is that there is some concern; my training and equipment lists reflect it. But my opinion is that the risk is well worth the result: solitude—man in the saddle, suspended between heaven and harsh environment. In this state many hours can go by without a passing car, with lazy, circling hawks and wide-eyed, staring deer your only company. And when you tire of them, or begin to feel the need for human company, you can always pedal hard for the next town, or hail a rancher, fill your water bottles, and discuss his concerns.

Then there are group tours. Constant society. People pressure. All the requirements of Locke's social contract, with much given and little gained. Nevertheless, some people like them, and the Fates will likely conspire to involve you in one even if you decide that solo is your style. If this happens, remember that the weakest rider determines the day's progress. On a group tour an individual's physical condition is no longer his concern alone. Long before the trip agree on how many miles you wish to average, then take practice tours to test physical and mental stress.

Between these extremes of solitude and society is the "partner" system. Much more workable than group tours, you can share the weight of community equipment in the following manner:

Slower rider	flashlight/batteries
tools	rope
all medical supplies	ripstop repair tape
chain links	safety pins
air gauge	sewing kit
air pump	can opener
	fingernail clipper
Faster rider	nail brush
tent	waterless hand cleaner
ball bearings	soap/soap dish
bearing grease	deodorant
oil	shampoo
lock/cable	candle holder/candles

In *Living* I've provided the following equipment lists and an explanation of each item's purpose and cost. While it may at first seem impossible to pack such an array of gear onto a single bike, you'll lessen the difficulty by keeping heavy items low and close to the frame, and by using front *and* rear panniers. Too much weight in a handlebar bag can throw off your steering; lower it to the front bags, and use this rough weight-distribution guide: three-fifths full weight in rear panniers and on rear rack, two-fifths on front rack, in front bags, and in handlebar pack.

Touring Checklist
Clothing:
T-shirts (3)
long-sleeved shirt (1)
riding shorts (2)
belt (1)
undershorts (3)
long pants (1)
gym shorts (1)
insulated underwear (1 pair)
Protogs (1 pair leggings)
socks (3 pairs)
riding shoes (1 pair)
camp moccasins (1 pair)
bandanas (2)
riding gloves (1 pair)
baseball cap (1)

Foul and cold weather gear:
boots (1 pair)
neck gaiter (1)
wool cap (1)
jacket (1)
gloves (1 pair)
poncho (1)
rain chaps (1 pair)
rain suit (1)
rain cap (1)
rain boots (1)
goggles (1)
down or fiberfill jacket (1)

Tools:
crescent wrench (1)
screwdriver (1)
needle-nose pliers (1)
channel locks (1)
tire levers (2)
allen wrenches
cone wrenches (2)
chain rivet tool (1)
spoke wrench (1)
freewheel tool (1)
cotterless crank removal tool (1)
Swiss Army knife (1)
pocket vise (1)

Shelter and bedding:
tent (1)
sleeping bag (1)
ground pad (1)

Personal:
towel (1)
washcloth (1)
soap (1)
soap dish (1)
toothbrush (1)
toothbrush case (1)
toothpaste
comb (1)
toilet paper
deodorant (1)
shampoo (1 bottle)
waterless hand cleaner (1 tube)
nailbrush (1)
fingernail clipper (1)

Bike parts:
brake cables (2)
gear cables (2)
brake pads (2)
ball bearings
bearing grease (1 tube)
oil (1 bottle)
chain links (5)
tube (1)
tire (1)
shock cords (2)
spokes (6)
riding flag (1)
fenders
air pump (1)
air gauge (1)
luggage racks (2)
water bottles
reflectors
lock and cable (1)
rearview mirror (1)
tube repair kit (1)

Medical supplies:
- sunscreen (1 bottle)
- aspirin (20)
- snakebite kit (1)
- Desitin (1 tube)
- hydrogen peroxide (1 bottle)
- Band-Aids (10)
- butterfly closure bandages (6)
- combat bandage (1)
- gauze compress pads (4-8)
- gauze (1 roll)
- Ace bandages (2)
- petroleum jelly (1 tube)
- Benadryl (1 bottle)
- insect repellant (1 bottle)
- water purification tablets (1 bottle)
- moleskin/2nd skin

Miscellaneous:
- pocket knife (1)
- sheath knife (1)
- sunglasses/case (1)
- flashlight/batteries
- camera/film
- rope (15')
- ripstop repair tape (6")
- matches (1 box)
- notebook (1)
- book (1)
- pen (1)
- safety pins (10)
- sewing kit (1)
- cup (1)
- utensil set (1)
- can opener (1)
- panniers (1 set)
- pannier rain covers (1 set)
- pants clips (2)
- map (1)
- compass (1)
- candle lantern (1)
- candles (2)

To lessen this equipment weight (approximately thirty to thirty-five pounds total), some riders forego a tent. I've done this myself in the past, and sorely regretted it. (The insect world and rainstorms make for sleepless nights and miserable mornings-after.) However, you can lessen your weight and still acquire protection by using a bivy sack in place of a tent. There is the drawback of size—you can't move easily inside them—but for solo touring they're the way to go. And take a good sleeping bag. Far too often I've been awakened by the cold, and found no solace until sun-up.

I've discussed panniers in other books and articles, and have space here merely to suggest that you choose *very carefully*. Utah has her own manufacturer in Lone Peak, which produces excellent bags. A novel and highly practical design is available from Robert Beckman Designs (made for use with the extremely strong and rigid Bruce Gordon racks), while other well-constructed panniers are available from such companies as Madden, Kangaroo, Eclipse, Kirkland, Cannondale, and several more. Shop around. Like equipment lists, pannier selection is a highly personal matter.

For those of you completely new at touring, you might consider a first-time ride with a private bicycle touring company. I've now ridden with four, who conduct at least some of their tours in the state, and thoroughly enjoyed each trip.

Rim Tours
94 West 1st North
Moab, Utah   84532

The Road Less Traveled
HC 66   Box 33
Ashton, Idaho   83420

Backcountry Bicycle Tours
P.O. Box 4029
Bozeman, Montana   59715

Backroads Bicycle Touring
P.O. Box 1626
San Leandro, CA   94577

Beyond all the positive psychological reasons for touring, it is physically beneficial. To paraphrase a British physician's report on exercise, it must be "moderate, regular, continued throughout life, and sufficiently vigorous to bring on slight breathlessness." Cycling fits the bill. Inexpensive, good for you, yet fun—who could ask for more?

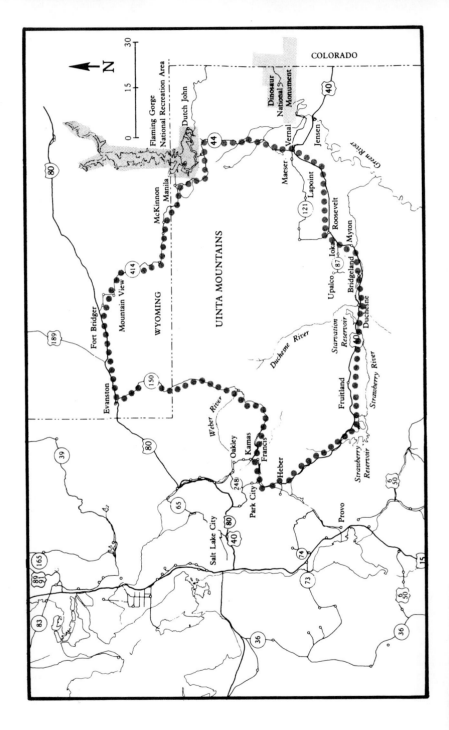

1. UINTA MOUNTAIN LOOP

HEBER—VERNAL—FLAMING GORGE— MANILA—FORT BRIDGER—EVANSTON— KAMAS—HEBER

Mileage: 480

Spur A	DINOSAUR NATIONAL MONUMENT	44 miles (roundtrip)	
Spur B	ANTELOPE FLAT	36 "	"
Spur C	RED CANYON VISITOR CENTER	6 "	"
Spur D	SHEEP CREEK CANYON	14 "	"

Mileage: 100

Of all the loops this is my favorite—a six hundred miler (counting spurs) which gives a taste of almost everything Utah has to offer. Add another ninety miles to that and you can begin and end in Salt Lake instead of Heber, which makes it perfect for a two-week, fifty-mile per day vacation.

One problem, however. To do this loop you'll have to be as tough as those whose trails you'll cross along the way: Dominguez and Escalante, the Spanish priests who in 1776 traversed the state; John Wesley Powell, whose

1869 trip down the Green and Colorado Rivers will be discussed in the next chapter; and mountain man Jim Bridger, within whose fort you'll have the honor of resting your weary bike and bones.

Those with a taste for rocks will not go wanting; there's a spectacular "Drive-thru-the-Ages-Geological-Area" on the way to Flaming Gorge, which you'll have to appreciate while climbing more than three thousand feet in twenty miles. (Don't be concerned. There are plenty of signs to explain the geology, and these make a great excuse to leave the saddle on the way up.) If you have an appetite for fish you'll likewise be sated, since you'll get to drown worms in four reservoirs, including Flaming Gorge National Recreation Area, numerous trout-stocked mountain lakes in the Uintas, and many other streams and rivers. You'll be so high at times that snow can come in August, and though there is no true desert on this run there is scrub so dry that you won't argue. Late spring through fall is best for riding; call the Forest Service or appropriate state agency if you're in doubt about the condition of mountain roads.

Along this loop there are red rock mountains which look like battleships in breakers, a summer alpine wonderland of cool breezes and cold nights, and wide-eyed deer to stare as you pedal past at sunup. There's also a cafe within each fifty miles, and with reservations you can motel your entire way around. But don't do it. Try the stars instead.

Although this loop begins and ends in Heber, many people will start from **Salt Lake**. Therefore, I'll begin with a quick route out of the city.

Those who leave from the University, Avenues, and central city areas of Salt Lake will find it best to use Emigration Canyon. This is done by proceeding east on Sunnyside Avenue (850 South) past Hogle Zoo and Pioneer Trail State Park. (Emigration Canyon is discussed in detail in Chapter Nine.) You'll begin with a moderate six-mile pull up the canyon—tough only in that it is fairly constant—and then ride a steeper final mile to the summit. There are two cafes on the climb up—Ruth's near the mouth and Crompton's about two miles from the summit. There is no shoulder and some fast (but light) traffic at times, so be careful. There's a lot of history here also, so be sure to glance at Chapter Nine.

Once at the top (known as Little Mountain), you have an excellent view of mountains in several directions, and a great two mile descent to Utah 65. Make a right at this point and drop another mile past Mountain Dell Reservoir to Interstate 80 and Parleys Canyon. Ride beneath the lanes (don't be misled by the road on the north side of I-80; it goes just past the Mountain Dell Golf Course and ends) and head east (uphill) on the I-80 shoulder.

Those of you who aren't starting from the north or central city areas need not take Emigration, though it's my preference no matter the point of origin. Your option is to join the Interstate near the Parleys Canyon Interchange on the far east side of the city. But let's be clear on this. I've talked at length with John Morris, Utah State Director of Transportation. He is extremely sensitive to cyclists' needs, and goes to bat for them several times a year when a new highway patrolman (also with the cyclist's best interest in mind) erroneously pulls a biker off a stretch of road which *isn't* off-limits. You must *not* be on I-80 west of Parleys Interchange, but you *are* allowed on the far right hand side of the shoulder from the interchange to Parleys Summit.

Those of you who come this way will have a five mile climb to the Emigration Canyon turnoff, and many cyclists make this short loop early on Sunday mornings before the traffic is heavy. Steep, rocky mountainsides along the interstate present a lovely view, and if you think the climb is tough give thought to the Mormon pioneer and church leader Parley P. Pratt, who built the first road up this canyon. (An easier route out of Salt Lake Valley, it avoided the difficult climb to Little Mountain.) He opened it in 1850, and charged a toll.

Okay, we're all on the shoulder of I-80 now, at the Utah 65 junction, our handlebars pointed east toward the summit some four miles away. If you aren't an experienced hill climber, and especially if this is your first time riding a loaded bike, the appearance of Parleys may scare you a bit. I find that many westerners have an erroneous conception of the relative discomforts of riding mountain ranges versus midwestern hills. With all due respect, except for some tremendous pulls in this state—Vernal to Flaming Gorge, Cedar City to the Breaks, Parowan to Brian Head—pedalling the nicely graded mountains is a snap compared to the never-ending steeper hills of my native Missouri. Few Utah roads are steeper than an 8% grade (an eight foot climb for every one hundred feet of linear distance), and most, like Parleys, are only 6%. Use your bike's lowest gears, talk to your friend or enjoy the scenery, and *don't* concentrate on how much farther you have to go to the top.

The summit is reached at milepost **(MP) 140**; but just a few hundred yards before this take the Parleys Summit Exit, putting you on the south side of the Interstate. There's a cafe here for a well-earned snack, and a phone to call someone to come and get you if you haven't trained sufficiently. (What's sufficient? Exactly that amount of previous riding—with all tour weight—necessary to pull such hills and still enjoy them.)

And a final word on canyon climbing before we pedal on. You will sometimes encounter "canyon winds" which make otherwise easy climbs a real bear. These winds generally, but *only* generally, move down a canyon to the valley below in morning, back up in afternoon. Personally, I don't try to plan around them, for something as inconsistent as canyon winds will keep you second-guessing till you're batty. On another level, wind is part of the package a biker bites off when he chooses his mode of travel, and it's as much a piece of the landscape as forests and mountains and clouds. Simple acceptance is the key.

The east-west road (immediately south of the Parleys Summit Sinclair station) paralleling the Interstate is first called Kilby Road as it descends eastwards from the summit, then changes to Frontage Road after a mile or so. Remain on the south side of I-80 for the entire four miles to Utah 224. This is Kimball Junction, named for William Kimball, who operated an Overland Stage stop.

And now another choice of routes. You can at this point turn south on 224 for an easy (though toward the end constant and gradually uphill) seven mile ride to Park City, or continue on frontage roads to U.S. Highway 40. The Park City road is unfortunately narrow and mostly without shoulder, but is seldom very busy.

Park City has a great attraction for many Salt Lake bikers, who pedal up and back on weekends along the route I've just described. A combination of the resort flavor of recent developments, and the historic "old town" remains of the mining era provides a distinctive difference from nearby communities. You'll have to look hard to imagine the place in the 1880s, when as a mining town it housed more than a hundred Chinese laborers. The city's 7,000 foot altitude makes it considerably cooler than Salt Lake, and with its numerous motels and restaurants provides the weary cyclist a welcome layover. If you prefer to camp, return to Kimball Junction, proceed north across I-80, then turn left (west) on the north-side frontage road and ride a couple of miles. This private campground can be reached more directly from Salt Lake by riding north under the Interstate at the Ranch Exit, a couple of miles east of Parleys Summit, then heading east on the more poorly paved north-side frontage road.

Should you decide to avoid Park City, ride north across I-80 from Kimball Junction on the overpass and turn east on the frontage road. You'll remain on the north side of the Interstate for only a mile or so, when the road hooks right (south) back under I-80. Make this turn and stay on this road as it continues to head east, then angles to intersect US 40 one mile south of the Interstate. You encounter a couple of rough hills on 40 as you head south toward Heber, but only in the first five miles. After that it's a lovely, long descent into the verdant Heber Valley. You'll have a shoulder a good deal of the way, and quite a bit of fast traffic at your elbow. Beautiful scenery too, high mountains and a long green valley, with sage-covered hills on either side.

The mileposts begin again at the I-80/US 40 junction; three hundred yards before **MP 4** is Utah 248, which turned east from Park City. You'll cross your first railroad tracks just after this junction, so be careful. Bike tires on wet tracks are like yours truly on skis—put your money on a headplant unless it's slow speed and all caution. Don't ever lean your bike while crossing tracks, even if they come on a curve. Hit them at a right angle, *always.*

If the US 40 traffic is getting to you (avoid Saturday and Sunday afternoons, and early morning–early evening commuter times) turn off to the west on the two-lane road just before **MP 15.** A sign at this turnoff says "Midway and Homestead 5 miles." **Midway** is a small town from which you can follow the main road east to Heber; the Homestead is a restaurant-motel with a resort flavor. Horseback rides, natural hot springs, fresh-water swimming and a mineral pool are available, but I prefer by far the Sunday morning quiet meal and valley scenes in fall. At this point, you're only three miles from Deer Creek Reservoir and the campgrounds which service it. Ask about the roads to these in Midway if you're up for some dirt riding and don't mind adding several miles to your trail. But I'd suggest the lovely campground fifteen miles past Heber on Highway 40 instead. Heber also has many motels to choose from, especially on the south side.

Make sure you've got food enough in your saddlebags for forty miles when you leave **Heber,** for the only cafes between there and the Currant Creek Lodge (MP 59+) are now under the waters of Strawberry Reservoir. If you do spend the night in Heber you might take in the Railroad Museum and Pioneer Village, with its vintage Western town.

The first milepost south of Heber on US 40 is **MP 21,** but don't let me put you off by saying you'll soon begin a single climb which won't top out until almost MP 36—a long fifteen miles away. It's a gradual climb until MP 33, with a nice picnic site and great scenery on the way up. This is Daniels Canyon, and you'll enjoy watching the mountain walls close in around you as you ride. A lovely stream will keep you company, and there's ice-cold drinking water and restrooms at the Whiskey Springs Picnic Area just before **MP 27.** The quakies and oakbrush on the hillsides are soon replaced by evergreens, and I was lucky on my ride to spot some lovely birds playing in the trees. (I described these in detail to a friend who knows such things, and he identified them "tentatively" as the "Black-headed Grosbeak," "Rufous-sided Towhee," and "Common Bushtit." While my heart goes out to anything which trudges through life with a moniker like the last fellow, I prefer my own journal names of "western jay," "western robin," "western . . . ")

When I rode this loop in late August a sign greeted me near the top— "Loose Gravel/Prevent Broken Windshield/Advisory Speed 25 MPH." I think I was the only one who read it. Or maybe replacing a windshield is just less troublesome than dropping one's speed to twenty-five. I put on my sunglasses, hunkered down in my saddle, and wished I had the thicker brow of an earlier hominid.

Lodgepole Campground (named for the tall, erect pines used by Indians as teepee supports, and in which this camp is nestled) comes at **MP 34+,** and is wonderfully cool sleeping in summer. There are a couple of knee-saving level spots during the fifteen mile climb, and the cyclist enjoys either a wide shoulder or dual lanes on his ascent. The shoulder continues past the summit at **MP 36,** making it easy to enjoy the scenery as you zoom down the other side.

Just before **MP 38** the Strawberry River crosses the highway. You'll be surprised at how small it is. In fact, it's so slender that when I first rode by I thought people were fishing in a field. You'll run along the river over nice terrain to Strawberry Reservoir, past woolly black-faced sheep, their bells clanking and echoing off the nearby hills. One has passed from the Christmas smell of evergreens to the arid odor of sage in a single descent.

A couple of steep hills await before you reach the reservoir's eastern edge, but the view of the water from their summits makes the climbs worth it. A sign at water's end points south to Soldier Creek Dam and Aspen Grove Campground. It is here that the countryside completes the transformation from alpine to junipers, and red and brown rock mountainsides.

I pulled off to read the historical marker on the northeast edge of the reservoir, and once again encountered a problem endemic throughout the state—missing plaques. The titles are present, but in many places only the mount remains. Whether the glue was insufficient to hold the metal tablets, or if their exits were assisted by vandals, I've been unable to learn. Nevertheless, since the marker in this instance sports only the title "Dominguez and Escalante," I'll fill you in.

In late July of 1776 Francisco Atanasio Dominguez and Silvestre Velez de Escalante, both Spanish Franciscan priests, left Santa Fe on what was to be an extraordinary five month, seventeen hundred mile expedition through the uncharted wilds of New Mexico, Colorado, Utah, and Arizona. Their stated purpose was to find a route from Santa Fe to Monterey, California (another Spanish settlement), and to proselytize among the natives along the way. With a handful of fellow Spanish and several Indian guides they entered Utah east of Vernal, roughly paralleled US 40 to the present-day marker at Strawberry Reservoir, and continued west to the site of Provo on Utah Lake.

At this point the padres turned south, and encountering snow near Milford on October 8, decided against proceeding to California. On September 21, 1776, when they led their horses past the site of the monument in question, Escalante wrote:

> Then we went down to a medium-sized river [now engulfed by the Reservoir] in which good trout breed in abundance, two of which Joaquin the Laguna killed with arrows and caught, and each one must have weighed more than two pounds. This river runs to the southeast along a very pleasant valley with good pasturages, many springs, and beautiful groves of not very tall or thick white poplars. In it there are all the conveniences required for a settlement. We named it Valle de la Purisima.

They had awakened that morning to ice in their cooking pots—a warning to bring a good sleeping bag if you're traveling in fall. We'll drop in on the fathers from time to time as we move about the state, to read their journal entries for an earlier view of the countryside.

You've earned the easy pedalling beyond the reservoir; my own journal speaks of pleasant miles, of different colored layered rock in hillside cutaways, and brilliant yellow Golden Aster flowers and rabbitbrush along the roads. Cold drinking water pours from a pipe at **MP 57+**, and two miles further is the Currant Lodge and Cafe. Stands of cottonwoods line the banks of nearby Currant Creek, and when I pedalled through in late August I had a taste of approaching fall. A farmer was burning leaves, and the delicious scent was drifting across the road.

At **MP 63+** comes the **Fruitland** General Store. It's twenty-five miles to the next town, and though it's gentle terrain you never know when the wind will change, sap your strength, and make you very hungry. No matter the season or locale I try always to carry a front pannier of food: bread, fruit, cheese, peanut butter, and jam. Also, don't count on general stores in small Utah towns to be open on Sundays. Stock up in Heber and carry the extra weight if you have to, but don't get caught short in this state.

Relatively easy, rolling terrain is yours to Duchesne and beyond. It's rock and juniper and piñon pine all the way; the mountains are past, and mesas lie in the distance. There is green wherever there's moisture, but reservoirs out in the dry come on with a shock, such as the bright blue face of Starvation Reservoir at **MP 82**. (You'll find drinking water before this, at a rest area at **MP 70+**, and picnic tables in the shade.) A lovely bridge takes you across the Strawberry River to the reservoir, near which two campgrounds sit: the CamperWorld next to the highway, another on the lake's northeast shore. Shaded picnic sites are just across the bridge, and there's a historical marker telling of the Spanish Fathers' difficulty in moving (westward) up Strawberry River Canyon.

You might be wondering why we haven't gone in the opposite direction— from Heber to Kamas and Fort Bridger, then west on US 40, especially in view of the upcoming massive climb from Vernal to the Gorge. An answer lies in Escalante's journal (they camped only a mile above Duchesne): "We arrived very tired, both on account of the day's march's painful travel and because a very cold west wind did not cease blowing very hard all day long."

The wind is the reason; for it usually blows west to east along this stretch, and can really get going in country where there is little to slow it down. This way you'll be in mountains when you head west, where the wind is less a factor.

Even with the shoulder you might be hassled by the traffic on Hwy 40, but keep a stiff lip; you'll be off it soon. Some of you have probably been looking wistfully at the alternative route of Utah 208 north to Utah 35. Don't do it. Utah 35 is unpaved.

You'll ride past the reservoir and drop into the little town of **Duchesne (MP 87)**. This place has restaurants, grocery stores, laundromats, motels. Live it up.

When you pull out don't jump back on US 40. Instead, one short block east of town, where the main road jogs south a bit, you'll see a two-lane paved county road coming in from the east across a bridge. Take it. You'll avoid the next twenty-three miles of Hwy 40 and endure far less traffic.

Just across the bridge is another marker on the wandering padres; this one is entitled "Father Escalante," and calls him "the priest." It should be noted that Dominguez was actually in charge of the mission and bore ultimate responsibility for it. Somehow that fact was ignored when names were bestowed on Utah towns and geographic features. You'll be pedalling through Escalante (drop the last syllable if you want to sound "local") on Loop Two, near the Escalante Petrified Forest, Escalante Mountains, Escalante Canyons.... But if I've ever pedalled past anything named "Dominguez" I was sleeping at the time.

Our county road runs along water all the way to **Bridgeland** (nine miles), and is therefore very green. It's also level, and reminds me of Midwest country lanes. You'll come to an LDS church on the left, and then another county road angling north. It's yours. If you miss it you'll come to the Bridgeland Post Office (no store in town). Bridgeland is the site of a former (1934-1939) Civilian Conservation Corps camp, one of Franklin Roosevelt's New Deal "alphabet agencies" which ultimately employed some half-million young men in projects such as flood control and reforestation.

Follow this north county road for about eight miles, over a couple of rough climbs, to its junction with Utah 87. One can catch glimpses of the Uinta Mountains now and again, a snow-capped range unique in North America in that it runs east-west. You will soon have a close-up look at these high mountains (with many peaks over 13,000 feet), for this loop circumnavigates the range until, south of Evanston, you pedal into them. Ride level Utah 87 east eight miles past lovely old fieldstone barns and houses, to its junction once again with US 40. From there it's a noisy and unpleasant five mile run into **Roosevelt** (cafes, grocery, motels), but at least there is a shoulder.

You'll notice the "oil money" influence on the main drag, the loud traffic of huge new four-wheel-drive trucks cruising along at twelve miles to the gallon—their beds empty, with only solitary young men behind the wheels. Cowboy hats and John Deere caps cocked back on sun-burned foreheads, a beer can in the hand, these fellows hail from all over North America. I spent a night in town talking to some of them, and the next morning as I pedalled out decided that I'd visited a latter-day Sutter's Mill. Home towns were boring; jobs were scarce; it beat the Army; good pay—all were reasons for moving to this dusty Utah town named for the stocky little fellow with pince-nez glasses—Theodore Roosevelt. He was a man who would have been at home with them, who would have shared and delighted in their energy. And he would have seen their motivation for leaving home and coming here as simply the American urge to be on the move and get ahead.

US 40 actually comes into town from the south; it takes off due east at the major intersection, while Utah 121—the road we want—veers off to the left. The ten miles north to Neola are fairly level (after an initial hill); you'll have a narrow shoulder and little traffic, and also a better feeling about Roosevelt as you pedal through its residential northern edge. Here, north of town, is a sign for "Blackpowder Ranchettes." Perhaps the name just came about for lack of something better, but it probably refers to the nearby site of Fort Robidoux—inhabited when black powder and flints were necessary items for the mountain man's self-defense. A half-mile east of Roosevelt—on US 40—is a historical marker:

Fort Robidoux: The first year-long abode of white men in what is now Utah was Antoine Robidoux's Indian and fur-trading post Fort Winty or Uintah, which was built eight miles north of here in 1832. It was on the trail from Taos, New Mexico to the Pacific Northwest, and from Utah Lake to the Platte River region. Many trappers traded and wintered here. Several distinguished travelers sojourned here including Kit Carson, Joseph Williams, Rufus B. Sage, Marcus Whitman, A.L. Lovejoy, and John C. Fremont, all prior to the burning [by Ute Indians] of the fort in 1844.

And now back to **Neola**, ten miles north of Roosevelt. Make a right at **MP**

10 and follow Utah 121 as it winds its way to Vernal; but if you're hungry there's a grocery store and cafe in Neola. Where 121 heads east, proceed north across the intersection a half-block; both services are on the left. (And both are closed on Sunday.) The road east of Neola is very good, with a shoulder, little traffic, and some old pioneer-type cabins before the little town of **Lapoint (MP 23+)**. Winn's Grocery is here, and the beginning of a rough climb to the edge of dry-bed Twelvemile Wash. Fill your water bottles for the fifteen miles to Maeser, for the hot sun and brilliant red rock in the wash looks and feels like southern Utah. From Neola to Lapoint the lovely southern edge of the Uinta Mountains looks cool and serene; but from there to Flaming Gorge the rock and dust and junipers will make you feel pretty dry. Fantastic landforms are in store for you beyond Lapoint—enormous plates of rock jutting hundreds of feet into the air, like the backs of armored dinosaurs; marine fossils that testify that what you see was under water at one time; multi-colored layerings along rock-faced walls. Slow down and enjoy yourself.

The residential outskirts of **Maeser** begin at **MP 34**; but it's not until **MP 37+** that you can slake your thirst. Just beyond the road curves south and joins with US 40 in **Vernal**. After so long communing with the rocks this busy town might scare you. Ride carefully. Proceed south across 40 two blocks and you can visit the 1901 Tabernacle and Daughters of Utah Pioneers (DUP) Museum—housed in Vernal's first tithing office. ("Tithing" refers to the payment to the Church by individual Mormons of one-tenth of their incomes.) Or, turn left and ride east on 40 a few blocks to the sign "Hwy 44/US 191"—after Western Auto, before First Security Bank—for Flaming Gorge.

SPUR A—DINOSAUR NATIONAL MONUMENT
(44 miles roundtrip)

But spend some time in Vernal first (many motels, and several nearby campgrounds along the road to the Gorge), and at least take in the Dinosaur Museum. This sits on the north side of US 40 two blocks east of the Gorge turnoff. If you plan to visit Dinosaur National Monument it's a level fourteen mile ride east on US 40 to Jensen (restaurant, no motels), then a bit of climbing six miles north.

However, depending upon weather conditions a second route is available. Proceed through Vernal on Main Street (US 40); on the east side of town is the Vernal Police Station. Turn north at the Station and ride approximately one mile, to the first four-way intersection. A two-lane paved county road heads east from this intersection for eleven miles, to its junction with Utah 149. Turn north on 149 and proceed to the Monument. (This alternative county road runs east from Vernal to 149 through the Buckskin Hills, then parallels Brush Creek for five miles. When water is high the road is impassable; inquire at the police station before heading out.)

Dinosaur National Monument has two campgrounds and much scenery—river gorged canyons, rugged juniper-covered hills, and landforms which silently echo the awesome geologic forces which created this area. But the best treat at this Monument is the Visitor Center Quarry. Block-faulting has tilted the rock wall of dinosaur fossils out of the ground; thus visitors can observe the on-going excavation of bones.

The bones of fourteen species of dinosaurs have been unearthed in this vicinity, and the huge models of these beasts at the excellent Vernal museum will assist you in imagining them lumbering about some 140 million years ago. Even if you're untrained in geology you'll soon be able to spot the distinctive dull gray Morrison Formation rock strata which denotes the "thunder lizard" time. You'll pedal past it elsewhere in the state, but it's in the vastness of the region north of Vernal that I can most easily imagine them, tall as buildings, dumb as fireplugs, moving lazily about, munching on plants and each other.

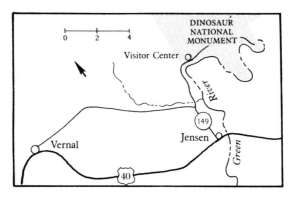

But enough of this. On to the Gorge. For weeks this massive, switch-backed mountain face has preyed upon your mind. Come on. No one cares if you walk the bike a bit. Cyclists ought to make their goal getting to the top; *how* they get there ought to matter less.

We're back in Vernal. Downtown. First National Bank intersection. Go north. You'll pass cafes and campgrounds in the first few miles but don't let the name of the last diner get to you.

Mileposts begin again; the sign says forty-one to Flaming Gorge, Manila sixty-two. It's a short steep climb past **MP 3** to Steinaker Reservoir, and again the brilliant blue water is a refreshing contrast to the redrock all around. I passed a nice half-hour with a fellow in his sixties, a fisherman who cried out "Want a coke?" as I pedalled by. He told me that nearly twenty years before, Lady Bird Johnson had dedicated this area. Looking around, I asked him what she'd said. He didn't know. He'd been fishing.

I started up the hill again, the sixteen-ounce soda sloshing about inside. In Vernal I'd lapped up a chocolate shake and many cups of coffee, sitting in a booth by myself thinking of the climb, and trying not to cry in public.

I thought of the dead dinosaurs. I thought of the late President Johnson. I read the signs along the road explaining the geologic ages I was passing through. Fossils of dead squid. Fossils of dead fish. It was a little depressing. Rather than excitement at this window to the past, I thought forlornly that this area was a veritable Gettysburg for all that slithered and swam and stomped about millions of years ago. I felt like I'd been drafted.

The switchbacks begin at **MP 12**; it's a rough 8% grade for a long way, so take it easy and make sure you've got enough water for the climb. There's an open pit phosphate mine on the way up (**MP 14+**), and even though there's no shoulder for most of this hill, the road is wide enough for an occasional truck to pass. After a few miles more comes a welcome geologic turnout—high enough to enjoy the cooling breezes while you sit and look below. Two enormous rock formations miles to the south recall the image of battleships crashing through million-year-old stone waves. The sign here reads: "View of the Past: Through the ages twelve different oceans abounding with life covered this area. When waters receded tropical plants, dinosaurs, and other creatures flourished... it took 200 million years to create this landscape." Someone, referring to the phosphate mine, has scribbled below, "And it will take the miners only *1* year to wreck it!"

Near **MP 18** comes a quarter-mile downhill, then the first summit at **MP 20**. A quick descent, then gradual climbs, and now you've traded red rock for thick stands of aspen and evergreen. The contrast is magnificent. It was a scorcher the day I made the climb, and on top of all the liquids I'd consumed in Vernal (and the coke) I drank more than a gallon coming up. (I pack 140 ounces)—almost nine pounds—of water on summer desert rides.) Huge gray-white clouds moved overhead, so different from the speckless blue I'd seen the days before. It was wonderfully cooler than down below, and when I finally reached the true summit 8428' (Vernal is 5331') near **MP 26+**, I had to stop and don a hat. (Each three hundred foot elevation rise drops the temperature about one degree Fahrenheit.)

The moisture in the air carried the romantic fragrance of Christmas tree lots, and as I circled one green mountain bowl a large white horse stood stonelike, watching me. He never moved his head a bit, but kept me in his huge brown eyes and snorted once or twice. When he did, tiny clouds of condensation formed before his great nostrils.

Thunder and lightning broke from the darkened clouds ahead, setting the stage for the inevitable afternoon mountain shower. I pedalled to another bowl, ringed with evergreens and filled with grass and yellow glacier lilies. Three hundred sheep stared back at me, a soft tinkling sounding from their bells as they moved their heads to get a better view. This sound, the wind through the trees, and the low-pitched bleating of the sheep each time the thunder rolled are all I heard in miles of alpine riding.

SPUR B—ANTELOPE FLAT—(36 miles roundtrip)

At **MP 30** is the first of two campgrounds, and the first opportunity for water in twenty-seven miles. An intersection comes at **MP 34+**; Utah 44 continues west (left) toward Manila twenty-eight miles away. If instead you ride northeast on Hwy 260, it's a fast six mile drop to Flaming Gorge Dam and the Visitor Center of the National Recreation Area. But partway down—at **MP 2** (mileposts begin again at the intersection)—is the Flaming Gorge Lodge, open year-round. Don't expect the great old log and shingle-roofed lodges of Yellowstone; this is more a modern, clean motel. The friendly lady inside suggested reservations be made in advance, and also told me that all these roads—back to Vernal, out to Manila and on up to I-80—are kept open in the winter. (The south-facing switchbacks get plenty of sun.)

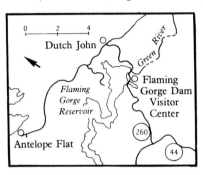

The road climbs sharply (but for less than a mile) after the dam; camp-grounds are found before and after the Visitor Center—inquire there about availability. At **MP 8+** is the **Dutch John** store and cafe, and on the next hill a sign saying "No Services Next 66 Miles." (If you think *that's* something, wait till Loop 4.) At **MP 10+** is the turnoff south for the Mustang Ridge Campground, a hilly mile-and-a-half run through lovely green countryside. But the view of the Gorge here, though reminiscent of a Midwest swimming hole, lacks the grandeur of Antelope Flat. This is purchased by another eight mile ride west; hilly at times, it is made acceptable by the scenery, the campground at the Flat, and the stalwart antelope which stand their ground as you pedal by.

SPUR C—RED CANYON VISITOR CENTER
(6 miles roundtrip)

Return to the intersection of Utah Hwys 44/260, and ride west. After four miles—at **MP 38+**—you'll come to a three mile long level road which runs north to Flaming Gorge Red Canyon Lodge and Visitor Center. (Four public campgrounds are in the vicinity.) Inside the Center is a huge glass wall through which is seen a spectacular view of the canyon fifteen hundred feet below. The lodge rents tiny cabins, but its excellent and inexpensive restaurant is its finest feature.

I camped near the lodge that night, and at dusk walked to the canyon rim. After climbing over the safety retainer wall in the growing darkness, I sat among the trees as the water turned black below me. Less than sixty miles to the north, and a century ago in time, one-armed John Wesley Powell left Green River to float past this spot on his way to the Grand Canyon. We'll meet up with him later and pry open his life and journal, but in the silence I imagined the four tiny boats and ten brave men, bobbing in the unknown waters.

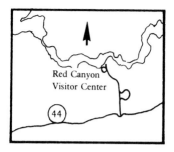

I awoke the following morning to a tent wet with dew, and pedalled off toward **Manila** with only the early sun and an occasional deer for company. The Blue Penstemon flowers gave a regal hue to the woods of pine and Douglas fir, and at **MP 41+** I spied a treeless mountain covered with snow. The air smelled of evergreen again, and I looked forward to a breakfast of hotcakes and coffee in town.

I almost didn't make it. Rolling down a quick, curving descent I let my eyes remain too long on a lovely alpine pond. As I admired it I sailed, unknowingly, into a herd of cows. The trick with bovine traffic is to yell before you hit them, as they will scatter in every direction and clear the lane. But wait until you're upon them and they're liable to scatter *over* you.

SPUR D—SHEEP CREEK CANYON—(14 miles roundtrip)

From the Red Canyon turnoff to Sheep Creek Canyon (MP 57—some nineteen miles) the terrain is a series of fast, long descents and slow climbs. Look at the map. You can see that the Sheep Creek Canyon Spur makes a half-moon loop off Utah 44 to the west. Your choice is to proceed north on 44 and ride a portion of the spur back south, or enter the south end of this loop and ride it north to its junction with the main highway. My preference is the first, for the latter plan causes you to miss the most lovely seven miles of 44, including one view of the Gorge (while flying down a mountainside) at **MP 54+** that you'll never forget.

You'll see signs for campgrounds as you pass, but on both my visits there was no sign for the north extension of Sheep Creek Canyon Road. No problem. Make a left on the little road that comes in from the west at the stream (Sheep Creek) just before **MP 57**. As you can see on the map, you can ride the entire eleven mile loop back to 44, then pedal once again the seven miles to MP 57, or simply go up a bit and return. I suggest you ride up only five miles, to a small memorial park, then turn around. You'll see the amazing rock formations, wonder at the isolation of a fellow who home-steaded this canyon in the 1880s, and read the sad tale of seven lives lost in a flash flood in 1965. (Remember this memorial when folks in Utah warn you not to camp in dry washes.) There are three stretches of unpaved road up to the memorial, but the longest is only a half-mile. And if you turn around where I suggest, you'll avoid the steepest part of the canyon climb.

Return to Utah 44—at the north end of the Sheep Creek Canyon Road. Ride north (over a couple of steep pulls) for six miles, to the small town of Manila (grocery, cafe, motel). A nice cafe sits at the junction of Utah 44 and 43; turn right at this point and proceed east on 43 for a block if you need groceries. Two miles east of town on 43 is a Flaming Gorge National Recreation Area campground and marina. (While eating breakfast in Manila I asked a waitress how the town had come to be so named. She didn't know, but the cook said it originated from the town having been laid out during the 1898 Spanish-American War—when Admiral Dewey captured Manila in the Philippines.)

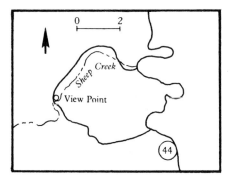

Manila sits near the mouth of a long canyon, and Utah 43 runs west on its north side until it comes to high, round mountains. The road jogs north at this point, and into Wyoming on State Hwy 414. Signs near the state line say "Lonetree 18, Mountain View 40," and it's only six beyond that to Fort Bridger. **McKinnon** and **Burnt Fork** have no services, and though I've ridden smoother roads there's pavement all the way, contrary to some state maps. This is all easy pedalling compared with what you've already done, and for that matter you've got easy riding until you head back up into the Uintas far south of Evanston.

Out ahead in this first Wyoming stretch there are tan colored rolling hills, divided now and then by strips of greenery wherever water runs. These streams have their sources far to the south, high up in the mountains, and as the day grew warm I stopped to wet my face. I had been told that **Lonetree** had a population of five, and a little general store. But when I pedalled in I found boards up in the windows, an ancient gas pump which would have felt at home with Model T's, and a sign: "The store has closed. We want to thank our many customers for all the years of patronage. Thank You. The Gregory Family 1897-1982."

Though none of the towns until Mountain View have stores or cafes, plenty of houses exist along the road—good for water and some company. I only stopped at one, and couldn't get away from those nice folks until I shared their lemonade, and packed a gift of oranges in my saddlebags.

Finally, forty-eight miles after Manila, I rode into the town of **Mountain View** (no motel). A warning. Eat at the cafe on the north edge of town, or stock up on supplies at the huge Thriftway and make a sandwich. Unfortunately, I went into the local drive-in, looking forward to a malt and burger after so many miles. What I found was more kids and noise and flies crammed into one room than I thought possible. And when I asked for a glass of water it cost me a dime—for the cup.

Three miles north of town, at an intersection where you'll make a left and head three more to Bridger, there is a convenience store, a laundromat, and the Gentleman's Steak House. There's another cafe on the way to Fort Bridger, and a couple more in town.

Fort Bridger is a little place, with two motels and a KOA, and a century and a half of history. Spend some time at the museum and you'll read of the fort in different periods: when it was built in 1842, how it served as supply post for emigrants on the Oregon Trail, when it was burned by the Mormons as Johnston's Army approached, then rebuilt as an Army post, Pony Express, and Overland Stage stop. Take some time to view the photos and think about the stream of humankind which passed before—by moccasin and hoof, with team-drawn wagons and handcarts, by steel rail and then paved road, and now you on a bike. Not last. Just next in succession.

In early morning I rode toward the interstate, past antelope and Canadian honkers. I finally heard the noise of I-80. Some state maps show a paved secondary road running parallel; I spent two hours taking every exit, only to backtrack when the access road dead-ended after a quarter-mile. You have no alternative to the nice, wide shoulder of the interstate, and only two long, low-gear pulls.

At the top of one of these hills is the Bingo station truck stop, with a sanitized "Fort Bridger Restaurant" attached. A raccoon had given its hide to dedicate the place, and hung stretched taut upon the wall. Photos and paintings of "appropriate" Western subjects abound. I sat drinking coffee from a styrofoam cup and eating powdered donuts, as a bored truck driver played "asteroids." The place was a world apart from Jim Bridger and his times, and in becoming a "period" restaurant had sacrificed the charm and function of a real truck stop. The hard-faced waitress who was everybody's mom and girlfriend to a few was gone, and with her went the link to society and female warmth which had welcomed the men by name. In this, and in the camaraderie of competitors who nevertheless understand and share one kind of life, the old-style truck stop had been exactly to drivers what Fort Bridger was to mountain men and emigrants.

Back on the interstate I nearly hit a guardrail while "baaaing" to some sheep. They'll speak sometimes, as will cows if you give a full, deep-throated moo, and mean it. Take the first exit for **Evanston**—the Interstate 80 Business Loop. You'll see the old brick homes and shops drawn up wagon train style, encircled against the onslaught of development. I made my way past new motels and fast food outlets, and found a place of incongruous name and cuisine—The New Paris Cafe. It was old, with a Wyoming easiness about it, and served oriental food.

It was good to sit quietly, away from the noise of traffic. I spread my maps across the table and plotted the climb back into the mountains—Wyoming State Hwy 150 south out of Evanston some twenty-three miles to the border, then alpine climes once again in the Uintas fifty-five miles to Kamas. From there an hour's ride to Heber.

Follow Main Street south to Wyoming 150, then past the giant Safeway, under the interstate, and on up the steep hill to the State Hospital and Women's Prison. Once past this hill it's easy, rolling terrain for miles, and you'll soon be free of the traffic which runs between Evanston and the suburbs south of town. Mileposts begin again. At **MP 8** you'll cross Bear River, fast-running as it cups the road, and coils now and then in pretty ox-bows. The mountains out ahead are lovely, and though you're high (Evanston is 6748′) you'll have to go much higher because the road snakes past the white-capped peaks. The final pass is Bald Mountain, at 10,600 feet.

Near **MP 10** is a marker on **Bear River City** (Beartown), which lived a short and stormy life, and then shriveled up.

Originally named Gilmer, Bear River City was founded in 1867 by timber drivers and their families working profitable logging drives on the Bear River. Union Pacific grader crews had arrived by October 1868, and changed the name to Bear River City. The population grew to about 2,000. Desperadoes and roughs soon took over the town. Citizens and mails were robbed, and people attacked on the streets in daylight. The vigilantes acted, and three men were hanged. This led to a riot in which 14 men were killed. The railroad pressed on westward, and by December 1868 Beartown was again a logging hamlet.

A sign at the Utah border (twenty-three miles from Evanston) says "Kamas 55 Miles, Mirror Lake 23." Bald Mountain Pass is only two miles south of Mirror Lake, and since this is your last summit of the loop it's downhill after that. Mileposts begin at fifty-five on the state line, counting down the miles to Kamas. (You're now on Utah 150.) Before the border the quakies come again, and at **MP 50** you're back in evergreens. Near **MP 48** is your last chance for groceries, a great little place called "Bear River Service." This cafe/store is open year-round.

Some rougher hills greeted me when I saddled up, and giant patches of snow lay in shaded spots. The place was wonderfully tranquil; every now and then a car, but mostly just the trees and me. Yellow columbine and mountain bluebells graced the forest floor, and every bird I saw seemed fat with winter feathers. Late evening, and on I climbed, losing light and growing colder in the rain that fell. I didn't want the day to end—my last full day of riding in a three-month summer tour. Christmas in August in the high hills, and I watched my breath form into ever larger clouds as I strained up the mountains.

Finally I pulled off into the pines and pitched my tent. The hail was kind enough to wait until I was camped.

You'll hardly have to pedal past **Bald Mountain** into **Kamas** (motel, store, cafe), but take the time to view the many overlooks. Four major rivers—the Duchesne, Provo, Weber and the Bear all begin here—and you'll have pretty waterfalls and rivers for the final downhill run to Heber. Follow US 189 south out of Kamas to **Francis** (store, cafe), then west along the Upper Provo Canyon in a quick descent back to US 40. From here it's nine miles south to **Heber**, or thirty-four miles north to Salt Lake.

*Consult Chapters Six and Nine for alternative routes from Kamas to Salt Lake.

It is hoped that cyclists are among the more environmentally aware travellers, but, as a reminder, I will quote from the guidelines and regulations established by the Bureau of Land Management for using the parks and recreational areas of Utah. (Ecological awareness and common decency would indicate that you try to observe these guidelines in all areas.)

Avoid activities that result in the disturbance of ecological relationships.

Keep campfires small and always under control; completely quench them when they are abandoned.

Carry out all wastes created by your visit.

Check the availability of potable drinking water or carry enough water for your needs.

Do not camp near watering facilities used by wildlife or livestock.

Keep all vehicles on authorized roads and trails.

Do not disturb Indian artifacts, pictographs, petroglyphs, ruins or other evidence of early cultures.

Do not collect petrified woods, fossils, gemstones, and rocks from any park, recreation site, forest or campground unless otherwise posted.

Observe all laws, including firearms and property laws.

Regulations vary according to season; check all regulations at the entrance of the area.

All parks and recreation areas are administered under the multiple use concept. Only through care and management—recognizing the delicate balance between the forces of nature—can we survive.

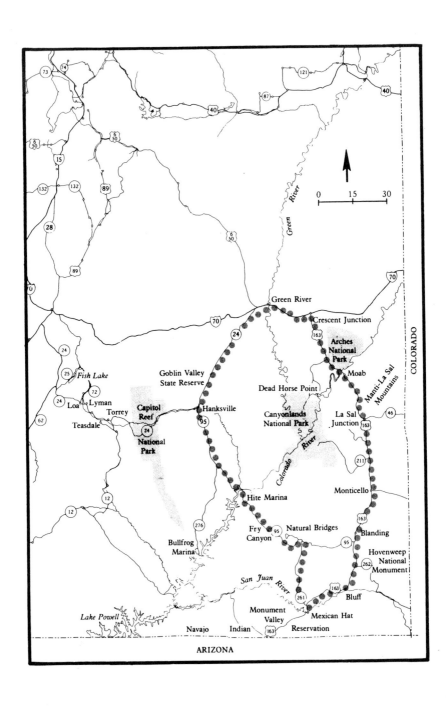

2. CANYON COUNTRY LOOP

GREEN RIVER—HANKSVILLE— MEXICAN HAT—BLANDING— MOAB—GREEN RIVER

Mileage: 379

Spur A	CAPITOL REEF/ FISH LAKE	192 miles	(roundtrip)	
Spur B	BULLFROG MARINA	84	"	"
Spur C	NATURAL BRIDGES	20	"	"
Spur D	MONUMENT VALLEY	52	"	"
Spur E	CANYONLANDS/ SQUAW FLAT	72	"	"
Spur F	NEEDLES OVERLOOK	42	"	"
Spur G	MANTI-LA SAL MOUNTAINS	60	"	"
Spur H	COLORADO RIVER	32	"	"
Spur I	ARCHES	42	"	"
Spur J	DEAD HORSE POINT	48	"	"

Mileage: 644

This enormous loop includes what most people envision when they think of Utah—colorful deserts, towering mountain ranges, huge rock arches and spires, and muddy rivers moving through steep-walled canyons. Though there are only two stretches of fifty miles or so without water, I still suggest early fall through late spring for the most comfortable riding (if you prefer, as I do, crisp nights and occasional light snow to days of broiling heat).

The region is a geologist's dream. The rest of us can also enjoy the strange configurations, and by reading the explanatory signs come close to imagining the incredible forces that have produced the varied landscape. But there's much more than just great formations. I had never before observed a desert in bloom, nor seen a greener area in the state than Monticello, at seven thousand feet elevation. Several times while sleeping in the sage and shad-scale (I carried no tent on this run) I was awakened when desert creatures scurried over me. In the cool of early morning I would follow their tiny tracks, past cactus flowers, bright yellow goldenaster, and Spanish bayonet. The birds that woke with me at dawn gave way to harmless bats at night, which more than once flew next to me for miles on desert rides.

The spurs are long, but worth it. Besides, upon having pedalled out in one direction I on occasion caught a ride back to the starting point, thereby saving hours for regions yet unexplored by me. Try it. It's done easily in a state which leads in per capita sales of pickup trucks and where people are at once friendly and incredulous that you're actually *pedalling* through the desert. Three national parks (Capitol Reef, Canyonlands and Arches) are made available through spurs, plus the Colorado River, the Manti-La Sal Mountains, and a lake at eighty-seven hundred feet elevation.

And history? We'll trace the movements of John Wesley Powell, the Army Major who lost an arm in the Civil War. We'll pedal the Old Spanish Trail, and the route of a Mormon colonizing mission which had to notch a rock to drive their wagons through. And finally, we'll cross the outlaw trail of Butch Cassidy on his way to Robbers Roost.

Loop One is my favorite, but this one is the real granddaddy of them all. Three weeks of fifty miles each day will cover it—the loop and spurs—and still provide for one long day of rest. Give it a shot; you'll come home having seen where "Fort Apache" was filmed—and feeling like the star.

If you drive to **Green River** to begin this loop, find someone who won't mind your car parked near his house for the length of time that you'll be on the road. I've done this in the past, and found it simple enough once I explained the circumstances. Choose a residential street with little traffic, then pick a door. Or, if you feel awkward, consult the local police about a good place to leave an unattended vehicle. Once this problem is solved return to Main Street and stock up on food and water, and go west.

In case you missed the town's historical marker on Powell's voyage, I'll add it here.

Major Powell—Colorado River explorer—First organized attempt to conquer the swirling waters and precipitous walled canyons of the Green and

Colorado Rivers was made by Major John Wesley Powell, Civil War hero and explorer. Warned by Indians and mountaineers they'd never return alive, Powell and nine companions started from Green River Station, Wyoming Territory, on May 24, 1869, with four boats, instruments for making scientific observations, and provisions to last ten months. For ninety-seven days Powell and his men battled the elements, enduring tremendous deprivation and hardship. One man, Frank Goodman, left the company early in the journey, and three others, William Dunn, O.G. Howland, and Seneca Howland, later killed by Shivwit Indians, deserted near Grand Canyon, Arizona. On August 29, 1869, the six remaining men, J.W. and W.H. Powell, W.R. Hawkins, A. Hall, J.C. Sumner, and G.Y. Bradley, arrived at the junction of the Rio Virgin in southern Nevada, having navigated and charted over nine hundred miles of the river. In May 1871, two years after his river voyage, J.W. Powell again led an exploring party of eleven men and three boats down the Green and Colorado Rivers. Well into 1873 members of Powell's party continued significant and important surveys of the region bordering the rivers traversed. The Powell surveys are some of the most significant explorations achieved anywhere in the world.

You have about thirteen miles of Interstate 70 to where Utah 24 cuts south, though I suggest you add another four or five miles west of the I-70/24 junction—up the long, gradual hill onto the San Rafael Reef. The view is magnificent, as from the vantage you can see into the uplifted area called the San Rafael Swell. Water has been the primary eroding agent responsible for the configurations in view, though this might seem difficult to believe if you've chosen summer for your tour, and stand, parched, looking at dry rock.

Try to prepare your mind for the upcoming ride by forgetting the pitiably short human time frame. Mankind (in one form or another) has been stumbling about for nearly three and a half million years. Human "civilization" is thought to go back only some five thousand years. You, as an individual, will be lucky to eke out the prescribed three score and ten. But the region you'll be travelling for the next few weeks—the Colorado Plateau—has been building up, layer by layer, for more than a *billion* years. Even if something took place only annually during that time period, like a spring thundershower, the cumulative effect would be enormous.

Turn back to 24 and head south. The road is long and dry (unless you're travelling in winter or spring); two wide lanes and a shoulder for much of the way combine with little traffic to provide hassle-free riding. In the forty-five miles to Hanksville from I-70 there are no very memorable climbs, and toward the end of this scenic run you'll drop down into town with delicious speed.

But a word about the surroundings. For the first twenty-four miles—from the interstate to the Goblin Valley turnoff—you'll have a reef to the west, a desert on the other side. The former is part of the rock formation completely encircling the uplifted "swell" area. This protective reef, as you can see, has been transformed by many tiny springs into a broken, saw-toothed chain.

To the east of Utah 24 lies what is called the Great Basin Desert. The name is used to differentiate it from the three other "kinds" of deserts in North America—those with different climatic conditions, and therefore variations in plant and animal life. The Great Basin Desert—which covers most of Utah, almost all of Nevada, and parts of seven other states—is caused by the "rain shadow" effect of the Sierra Nevada and Cascade Ranges. This refers to the movement of moisture-laden clouds from the ocean up and over mountain chains; as it rises the air mass cools, the moisture condenses, and falls on the western-facing slopes in the form of rain or snow.

Temple Mountain is in view to the west of Utah 24 as you approach the **Goblin Valley** turnoff. It has been claimed that the uranium used for the Hiroshima atomic bomb was mined here, and (in jarring contrast common to this state) the rider who takes the Goblin turnoff can view Indian pictographs on the way. Continue due west on this paved road up South Temple Wash and you'll see an area perfect for a few bikers to pitch a tent. There is a nice campground at the Goblin Valley State Reserve, as well as fascinating rock formations, but this comes after five miles of rough dirt road. (Water and shower facilities at the campground.)

One day soon I plan to "mountain bike" the roads which thus far have kept my touring bike at bay—those washboard trails far off the beaten path. Such a road heads southeast from the Goblin turnoff on Hwy 24 at a sign which says "Roost Flats 32." The Robbers Roost area served in the nineteenth and early twentieth centuries as a hideout for many outlaws, including Butch Cassidy and the Sundance Kid. Stolen horses and cattle were kept there until they could be transferred safely and sold. With their intimate knowledge of the rough canyon paths and desert waterholes the outlaws could easily escape the lawmen's grasp.

But enough of the wilds. Ride on to **Hanksville**, and luxuriate in the malt shop or motel. The town is small, but has everything a biker needs.

SPUR A—CAPITOL REEF/FISH LAKE—

(192 miles roundtrip)

And now comes the time to decide whether taking a spur is worth it. First, you don't have to ride all the way to Fish Lake; **Capitol Reef National Park** is only forty miles away, and though it has no services, there are campgrounds and many beautiful sights. Allow me to lure you there with a paragraph from a Park brochure.

Capitol Reef National Park lies in the slickrock [hard sandstone] country of southern Utah, an area where water has cut monoliths, arches, and mazes of canyons out of a sandstone-and-shale desert. The term "reef" as applied to land formations means a ridge of rock that is a barrier. This reef was named for one of its high points, Capitol Dome, that resembles the dome of the U.S. Capitol. Penetrated and explored only in the last 100 years, much of the park remains a rugged wilderness.

The road from Hanksville to the Park has only a few rough climbs and generally light traffic as it follows the Fremont River. Even if you decide against the Fish Lake extension of this spur I strongly suggest a ride to **Torrey** from the Park. (Two rough climbs.) After the fruit trees and greenery along the Fremont River, these red and brown rock cliffs and towering formations seem all the more spectacular. A few miles east of Torrey is the Rim Rock Motel, perched on a scenic ridge. In town are nineteenth century buildings with a rustic architectural charm. (Torrey also has a motel, store, and the Eagle's Nest Cafe on the west end where I've eaten many times. The dauntless proprietors were unfazed when I showed up once with a group of fifteen hungry high school cyclists, though an advance call is always appreciated if your group is large. Don't count on the cafe being open, however. It was closed the last time I pedalled through.)

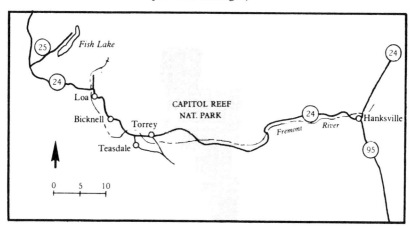

Should you choose to continue east, stop for a while in the tiny hamlet of **Teasdale**. Grab something cool to drink from the little store, then sit by your bike and listen to how *quiet* it is. If you're there in evening you'll see the ladies of the town out for a stroll; these tough, warm-hearted women in long skirts provide a softening element to the background of Cocks Comb Ridge and Boulder Mountain. I inquired once about the "bottle house" in town—a block east of the Post Office—a place with walls made of bottles which I learned was constructed by Tora Nelson.

More pretty countryside follows, on the way to a town which changed its name from Thurber when an easterner offered a library to any Utah settlement which would take his family name of **Bicknell**. It has two motels, a medical center, a couple of restaurants—one of which broke with tradition to serve me hotcakes long after the deadline for breakfast had passed.

An easy ride on to **Loa** (motels and restaurants), but then a monstrous 8% climb from the town at seven thousand feet and **MP 52**, to the summit at 8385', eleven miles away. You'll top out, then head down a mile to the **Fish**

Lake (Utah 25) turnoff, and then pull a more pleasant climb to the lake at 8700'. The Fish Lake Lodge is picturesque; one of the great Western inns of old. Built in 1933, the log and shingle-roofed structure has a dining room, grocery, cottage and cabin accommodations. Numerous campgrounds dot the sixteen miles of paved road from Utah 24 to the lake's northern edge. (The lodge is eight and a half miles from the junction of Utah 24 and 25.)

But now, back to the loop. It's twenty-six miles from **Hanksville** south to Utah 276—the Spur B Bullfrog Marina turnoff. The first two and a half miles out of Hanksville is a gradual climb, and from the top, the Henry Mountains are in view. These snow-crested eleven-thousand-foot peaks looked majestic as I cycled by in early summer, and I recalled on another ride three years before having seen them, white-shrouded, in early March. Buffalo, bighorn sheep and cougar are said to live in this area of colorful names— Ragged Mountain, Bull Dog Peak, Coyote Bench, and No Man Mesa.

SPUR B—BULLFROG MARINA—(84 miles roundtrip)

It was nearing 9:00 P.M. when I began the spur to Bullfrog. There was a stiff wind against me from the moment I left Hanksville. I had expected no difficulty in making it to water that night, and thus had only filled three bottles. Becoming drier by the minute, I decided to forego a thirsty sleep and pedalled in the dark to **Tickaboo**. This uranium mine "planned community" lies twenty-eight miles south of Utah 95, and twelve miles north of Bullfrog.

The ride is a scenic interplay of washes and canyons, sandstone and junipers. As the huge red sun dropped behind the mountains on my right, the desert awakened. Birds and insects appeared, and since there was no traffic I could clearly hear their energetic sounds. Soon it was too dark to see the bright flowers which had kept me entertained in the saddle, and in a little while I could barely see the road.

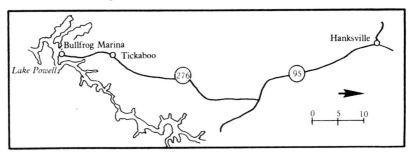

The moon rose slowly, giving a yellow glow to distant mountaintops to the east, while to the west the reddened slopes burned down, and then went out. Watching this, I felt as if I was at the midpoint of a giant compass. The wide-screen entertainment of the ancients then gradually unfolded. Trying to stay on the road and still spot the constellations, I raced past aromatic washes where ground water yet remained. I'd feel the coolness of the moisture first, then smell the sage and other desert plants, then lose them as the wash was passed and another hill began.

It was at the bottom of one of these sharp descents that I picked up a bat. Most cyclists have had the experience of birds accompanying them—from hawks to meadowlarks or wrens, and I had read that desert bats come out at night to feed on insects; but this reasoning at first did little to warm my heart to the ugly thing. He stayed about ten feet away, and when on my left— against the moon—reminded me of grade school and pictures drawn for Halloween. Then a second sentinel appeared. And, unbelievably, I rode escorted by those two bats for ten long desert miles.

Tickaboo appeared. I drank my weight in water, unrolled my sleeping bag, and fell asleep.

These were not the miners of old. Their faces lacked the exhaustion so apparent in photographs. They were as clean as Saturday morning fishermen, with ball caps and faded jeans and crisp voices at ease in the all-male atmosphere. Huddled over coffee cups, they employed curses as every possible part of speech in the carefree manner known to soldiers. Hard bodies and rough talk, but kindness ruled the heart. I'd slept behind the motel, asking no one's permission because of the late hour, and feared a rebuke. Some of the men had seen me as they walked to the cafe.

"You sleep okay, fella?"

"Bet he was cooler *outside* than we was *in*!"

"I'm just surprised the *snakes* didn't eat him."

The ribbing continued, breaking down the distance with each word. I ate my cakes and learned of mining, and introduced them to the world of modern bikes.

Similar ups and downs from Tickaboo to **Bullfrog Marina** at **Lake Powell**, but mostly down, to 3712′. I'm told the boat tours are fabulous, as the tiny craft explore the high, sheer red rock walls rising from brilliant blue water. The lake, created by Glen Canyon Dam in the 1960s, is two hundred miles in length, with a twisting shoreline of two *thousand* miles. Those of us who have never seen the geologic wonders covered by the lake have an easier time appreciating the beauty and recreational activities provided. Still, the nagging thought is there—what we're seeing is only skin deep. The spires, arches, deep-walled canyons, the views at which Major Powell marvelled as he floated past, the steps cut into solid rock by the Dominguez-Escalante Expedition more than two centuries ago, all these wonderful things and more are forever lost. The dam is in Arizona, the water in Utah; California gets the watts.

But, having no time for boat rides, I merely took a quick look around and jotted down my notes—motel, campground, restaurant, and a nice young lady named Annique in the marina gift shop.

I met a truck driver. It was fair, I figured. I'd already ridden the stretch *one* way; why couldn't I catch a ride back to Utah 95? After all, I'd save forty-two miles. And besides, who would care?

The ride south on Utah 95 from the Bullfrog turnoff is great through narrow water- and wind-sculpted red canyon walls. I passed Hog Springs Campground a few miles south of Utah 276, enjoying the wide shoulder on this "Bicentennial Highway" (paving was completed in 1976). The route of the North Wash from its collection points in the mountains to the Green River is what has made a path through the sandstone, and bright green plants line the colorful walls. It was a good descent in places, but my speed was slowed by head winds that whipped through the canyon. A high tower of red rock guards the first extension of bright blue water as you come to Lake Powell again.

The road then jogs north, crosses the backed-up waters of the Colorado, and comes to Del Webb's **Hite Marina** turnoff (twenty-two miles south of the 276/95 junction). From Utah 95 it's a relatively unattractive two mile ride west to the store (water, groceries), and another mile beyond that to the campground on the water's edge. But even with the extra distance don't pass it up, unless you've got water to make it another twenty-one miles to the Fry Canyon Store. It's pretty riding over rolling terrain from Hite to this last spot for supplies (grilled food and a few groceries).

When you leave Fry Canyon you'll pass a multi-million-year-old rock formation called Cheesebox Butte; these formation names are interesting in that some are now *themselves* outdated. I rode on, thinking of the obvious reasons for "cathedral" rock and "comb" ridge and others, and wondering what we'd name these things today. I was also expecting soon to catch up with two young women cyclists, who had reportedly left the Fry Canyon Store just a bit before my arrival. There was a lesson to be learned in the fact that during the next twenty miles—to the Natural Bridges National Monument turnoff—as I pedalled manfully up and down the hills, I never got close enough to catch a glimpse of them.

SPUR C—NATURAL BRIDGES NATIONAL MONUMENT
(20 miles roundtrip)

Natural Bridges National Monument is a must. You're only five miles from the Visitor Center as you turn off Utah 95, and most of it is downhill. An eight-mile loop from this point takes you past a great campground and a few of the world's most remarkable examples of water-erosion-created bridges of rock. Campgrounds were full; I wheeled off into the junipers, ate a can of spam beneath a star-brightened desert sky, and looked forward to an hour's pleasant reading with my tiny flashlight. I was fast asleep in two pages.

The next morning I completed the short loop, passed a wonderland of desert cactus in bloom, toured the Visitor Center, and returned to Utah 95. I contemplated heading back west a bit to Utah 263, to take the scenic and historic (Hole-in-the-Rock route) forty mile ride to Halls Crossing Marina (campground, groceries). But I decided against it, and proceeded east. (I did take this route on another trip to southern Utah, and found a great Anasazi cliff dwelling. But you'll have to be careful not to miss it. There are no signs for it on the road, so pay attention to the mileposts. One-eighth mile west of MP 13 is the dwelling—on the north side. A few miles west of this point you'll see the faint tracings of a dirt road a few hundred feet south of—and paralleling—263. This is a portion of the 1879-1880 Hole-in-the-Rock Trail.)

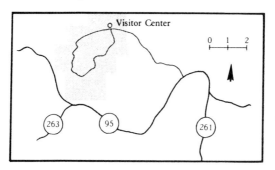

LOOP ALTERNATIVE

When you're at the junction of Utah 95/261 there is a good reason to consider your options. You can, as I did on my first ride through this area, continue due east another thirty-two miles, across Comb Ridge, past wide green fields near Butler Wash, and then do a hard climb into the pines. I'd been told by the ranger at Natural Bridges that I would "fly" to **Blanding** due to "all downhill and westerly winds." We'd read the same book of meteorology. The wind *was* supposed to blow from the west in these parts. But instead I fought a head wind for much of the way. And sure enough, two blessed "downhill truck signs" appeared—one said ten miles, the other two. However, the ranger-motorist had forgotten to mention the two-mile climb to the top of the comb, and a second rough one after that.

That is your loop alternative. Take it and head north to Blanding and you shave off fifty miles, not counting spurs. But you miss so much that I hate even mentioning it as an option. Instead, let's go back to the 95/261 junction.

Head south on 261 and you'll pedal hills of sage and juniper for twenty-three miles. But then comes a sight which would easily make *walking* that far worth it. It's called the Moki Dugway Overlook—a three-mile, twisting dirt road to the Valley of the Gods below. You're a thousand feet up and can see to South America, or so it seems. Some state maps show the first twenty miles of 261 south of 95 as unpaved; don't believe it. The only unpaved part is this dugway (the word, which you won't find in *Webster's*, refers to just this kind of twisting, fast descent), which is so washboarded and steep that you might have to walk. The "Muley Point Overlook" is gorgeous, and the five-mile dirt road should be traversed, if you're on a mountain bike.

Once at the bottom you have another six miles to US 163. Valley of the Gods is to the northeast; its spires suggest what's in store (in larger scale) at Monument Valley. One mile north of 163 is the turnoff for the San Juan River Goosenecks. This four-mile rolling, paved road heads west to the magnificent twisting river canyon—a thousand foot deep "entrenched meander." Camping is allowed at the overlook, but no water is present.

Finally, return to Utah 261 and head south toward the town which takes its name from a rock you'll see as you pedal in—a sombrero balanced on a beam. **Mexican Hat** has a store, restaurant, cafe, campground, and motel.

SPUR D—MONUMENT VALLEY—(52 miles roundtrip)

You're on the San Juan River now, the northern border of the Navajo Reservation. Proceed down the hill (on the west end of town), across the suspension bridge, and up a sharp climb, then through uneventful country-side for almost twenty miles until familiar sights appear. Not because you've seen them before; but because you've seen the incredible scenery of these enormous columns of rock a hundred times in old westerns, in documentaries on the West, in dogfood and car commercials. Another few miles south and you'll come to a paved road which runs west to Gouldings Lodge. There a campground, motel rooms, restaurant and store await the weary cyclist.

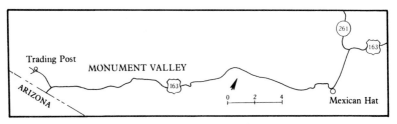

After returning to the 261/163 junction (three miles north of Mexican Hat), it's time to do the twenty-three mile run to Bluff. I found the riding a pleasant series of long grades up and down, with pretty countryside and light traffic. These were real American Southwest scenes—long vistas, huge buttes, rock points rising hundreds of feet from the desert floor, and one formation which looked exactly like a giant Hershey's Kiss sitting in a bowl of dust. Three miles south of Bluff is the **Sand Island Campground**, at which I stopped to dunk my head in the San Juan, and photograph the nearby petroglyphs.

Bluff has motels and a restaurant, and as I sat with my hamburger and malt I listened to the Navajos in other booths. Their voices were pleasantly subdued, the children mannerly. Tables of older Indians spoke only Navajo, while behind me a young man answered his much older companion in part-English sentences. Cowboy hats remained on their heads while eating, and jeans and boots and pickup trucks outside identified everyone but me. At the counter sat a gent who could have just stepped out of time. His wiry build, gravelly voice and long, waxed moustache genetically programmed him to be a town marshall.

I was reading about the Hole-in-the-Rock expedition. This dusty burg was the end of the trail for them. It seemed incredible.

It began with Brigham Young's colonizing program. In November of 1879 a group of 250 people in eighty-three wagons left the settlement of Escalante (you'll be there on Loop Three) for Bluff. There were obstacles: it was winter, they feared the Navajo and Paiute, more than two hundred miles of wagon road would have to be built over rock and desert, and they had to cross the Colorado River. Of course, crossing it wasn't all that difficult; a ferry would be built. It was getting *to* the river, down the fifteen hundred foot gorge which the Colorado had eaten into the land.

A natural slit in the huge rock lip of the gorge was found. It took six weeks to widen it enough for a wagon to pass through, and during this time, on the lower end of the notch, men hung by ropes to drill holes beneath a natural ledge, then inserted oak stakes as support for the brush and rock and gravel which they piled on top. In this manner a wagon road was built onto a cliff face. Finally, with teams of horses in front and humans holding onto the rear, the wagons were driven through the hole.

Thoughts of *that* expedition put *mine* more in perspective, and made it somewhat easier to pull the long hill out of Bluff. I rode the ten miles north to Utah 262, took it east for nine miles, and where 262 turned south I continued on the unnumbered paved road which heads east for another six miles over several steep hills. It looked like the moon, and then I rode another bend and saw a green oasis. A small adobe building lay nearly hidden in the trees. Talking with the proprietor of the **Hatch Trading Post** I learned that she had planted the trees twenty years before, and that they are watered by an artesian well. Peacocks strutted in the yard as we walked about. Restored by cold water and conversation, I headed out.

The pavement ends about three-quarters of a mile after the trading post, but I pressed on. I wanted very much to spend the night at **Hovenweep**—a national monument of twelfth century ruins, the former dwellings and ceremonial chambers of the Anasazi Indians (the Navajo word for "ancient ones"). There is a campground there, and in Mexican Hat I had met a couple from Holland, with whom I was to spend the evening if all went as planned. (The man intrigued me. He was doing graduate work in Arizona, and constantly marveled at the expanse of the West. "It's the first time," he said, "that I've lived lower than the *seventh* floor!") But I didn't make it. A mile and a half of teeth-chattering washboarded dirt road was all I could handle. I turned my heavily laden touring bike about, and pedalled west. (Don't miss it if you're on a mountain bike, however. I returned years later on an ATB and loved both the ride and the ruins.)

The fifteen miles to **Blanding** (motels, grocery, cafes) from the junction of 163/262 is not extremely rough, though a constant flow of traffic, a narrow shoulder, and my own slow speed due to climbs lessened my appreciation of the scenery. (An unexpected break lies four miles south of Blanding at the 163/95 junction—a well-stocked gas station/grocery.) Blanding's altitude of 6100', however (eighteen hundred feet higher than Mexican Hat), assists in making the area far greener than further south; the cultivated fields and warm farm smells were pleasant after so much rock. (See the "Edge of the Cedars" museum in town; next to it is an eighth-century Anasazi village.)

SPUR E—CANYONLANDS/SQUAW FLAT—(72 miles roundtrip)

From Blanding north to **Monticello** (motels, grocery, cafes) you'll climb another nine hundred feet over twenty-three miles, pulling some 7% and 8% hills and rolling constantly. The road cups the eastern edge of the Manti–La Sal National Forest, and climbs and twists through stands of pine, juniper and oak. It's a rough jaunt to Monticello, but I earned a fifteen mile downhill and level run from there north to Church Rock. This huge boulder (which looks more like a cookie jar) lies directly east of the Utah 211 turnoff west into Canyonlands National Park.

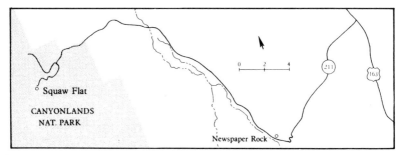

This is a hot, dry thirty-nine mile run one way, but very scenic. (Two lanes paved, little traffic, with only two good climbs.) Eleven miles in you'll pass Newspaper Rock, a flat slab face with a thousand years of carvings. (A few campsites here, no drinking water.) After this the road follows a stream, which means cottonwoods. On the day I pedalled out the air was filled with cotton tufts (to which the tree's seeds are attached), and though I couldn't avoid swallowing a few, they added to the charm of red ridgerock, old abandoned ranches, ancient corrals, and occasional flocks of sheep. The campgrounds at the end of this long Squaw Flat road are pretty, and do have water. (However, I was told by a ranger that one should call the Squaw Flat Ranger Station to determine if water will be present.) Though the ride is grand, I prefer the scenery at the end of the next spur to the north—the Needles Overlook.

SPUR F—NEEDLES OVERLOOK—(42 miles roundtrip)

Return to US 163, ride an easy seven miles to the Needles Overlook turnoff, and head west (23 miles, easy riding) through somewhat less scenic terrain than the Squaw Flat run. (The Wind Whistle Campground, on this road about five miles west of 163, is open from April through October. Again, inquire about water.) But the view from the overlook! You'll peer over thousand foot cliffs, across a forest of tall stands of rock like pencils in the sand, to tributaries of the Colorado before it joins the Green. No water here, or camping, though as always a sleeping bag in the trees, out of view of the road, is better than a cyclist on the highway after dark. (Of course, no open fires.)

Back on 163 again; **Moab** lies thirty-nine miles to the north. (This interesting name is biblical—referring to an ancient kingdom southeast of the Dead Sea, the same direction of present-day Moab from the Great Salt Lake.) The terrain is a series of long, very gradual climbs and descents. La Sal Junction (fourteen miles north of the Needles Overlook road) has a cafe, but you'll have to wait until Moab to really resupply. The town is the largest since Green River, and has all amenities.

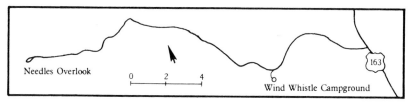

During the last twenty miles of your approach to Moab you'll have a huge, steep reef of rock on the west, the La Sal Mountains in the distance to the east, and in front of them a long, low green swath of fertile irrigated land. This is called Spanish Valley, and is part of the Old Spanish Trail. You'll encounter it elsewhere in the state (Loop Three) where historical markers tell of its importance as an early nineteenth-century pack trail from southern California Spanish settlements to those in New Mexico.

SPUR G—MANTI–LA SAL MOUNTAINS—(60 miles roundtrip)

Spend a night in Moab, then set your sights on the La Sals. These mountains are beautiful, and I had one of my most private days climbing into this truncated chain of twelve-thousand-foot peaks. State and section maps indicate dirt road all the way, but except for rough surfaces at the beginning and very end, and a half-mile of dirt at the top, it is completely paved.

Head south out of Moab on 163; on the outskirts you'll come to a Holyoak Realty Company on the west side of the road. It sits on Holyoak Drive, which angles east by southeast (you *are* carrying a compass with you, correct?) away from 163. After two miles you'll head down a slight hill and run into a crossroad. Holyoak ends; make a right so as to be heading south, and proceed a quarter-mile to another road which angles east-southeast toward the mountains. Take it, past Don's Diesel Repair and the Spanish Valley Vet Clinic. The land is now green due to the water of nearby Pack Creek. When you're fourteen miles south of Moab (you've been paralleling 163 thus far; the two actually connect three miles south of town) one road will turn due east into the mountains; the other will continue south to **Pack Creek Campground**.

Take the road into the mountains, and plan to climb for fifteen miles or so. It's beautiful, with flowers, fir, pine, and quakies shimmering in cool breezes. From the top you'll gaze at scenes which etch their place in memory. Castle Valley sits below; giant cones of rock with enormous towers on top. And just before the half-mile dirt road is a V-shaped wooden trough, driven into the rocky hillside and spilling out its cold water for passersby. (Two campgrounds are up here somewhere—both miles of dirt-riding off your path.

Again, my preference in such cases is sleeping in the trees, and avoiding the noise of radios and dogs in summer campground scenes.)

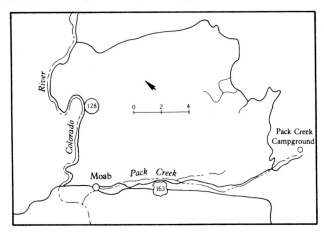

You'll drop off the other side, flying down the twisting road toward the Colorado River far below. Then it's sixteen miles of river riding on the easy, little used Utah 128, which snakes its way through canyon walls set off by cottonwoods. You end this spur back at 163, three miles north of Moab.

SPUR H—COLORADO RIVER—(32 miles roundtrip)

Another pretty stretch of river riding is Utah 279, which joins 163 five miles north of Moab. At the end is an ugly potash mine, at the beginning a uranium mill, but the sixteen miles between are all canyon walls and Colorado River. It's downhill to the mine, past Indian ruins (extremely hard to see—across the river and high on a ledge), and signs for petroglyphs and dinosaur tracks and a lovely "jug handle" arch on the side of a mammoth wall of rock. No traffic here, but no drinking water either for the thirty-two-mile roundtrip.

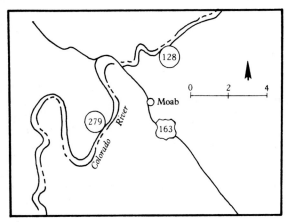

SPUR I—ARCHES NATIONAL PARK—(42 miles roundtrip)

Back to US 163 again. Two miles north up Moab Canyon, from the 279/163 junction, is **Arches National Park**. Spend a long time in the Visitor Center learning the geologic reasons for the wonders (and what wonders!) which lie over the hill. (And what a hill!) Then purchase the pamphlet "The Guide to an Auto Tour of Arches National Park." It will lead you to and explain the various formations, as well as show you which road to take to the campground fifteen miles from the Park entrance.

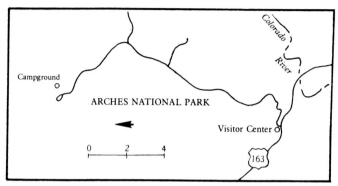

I won't spend any more time on this region (aside from the quick ride out to Dead Horse Point) due to the limitations of size and weight which I referred to earlier. But I want to make clear that my fast treatment of such wonders as the San Juan Goosenecks, Monument Valley, Delicate Arch and all the rest shouldn't create the impression that these beauties are not quite worth the ride. Listen to the languages you hear spoken in the parks; I've literally met people from around the world while pedalling Loop Two. They've come across the oceans to view what's at our door—a geologic carnival of rock. The fault lines and fractures, the uplifts, the grabens and entrenched meanders and a hundred other things you'll read about to try to understand—even when you've lost all this, you'll not forget the grandeur of the view.

SPUR J—DEAD HORSE POINT—(48 miles roundtrip)

Six miles of climbing north from the entrance to Arches, again on US 163, a twenty-four mile water-only-at-the-end, one-killer-of-a-hill road takes off west. A visitor center and campground with water will restore you at the end, but not as quickly as the view you've earned. If any sight is more panoramic than those described previously, this is it. The earth drops away forever, it seems, until somewhere below it meets at a right angle a huge expanse of colored rock that encompasses the river. The Colorado goosenecks its way slowly south from Dead Horse Point, carving ever deeper.

But there the show ends, I'm afraid. The twenty-one miles north on 163 to **Crescent Junction** (from the Utah 313 Dead Horse Point turnoff) are pretty bland, especially after having seen the Acropolis of rock. It's an easy, level ride, though traffic returns. Crescent Junction is a gas station, run by the roughest looking softie I've ever met. I guess I looked like I'd been baking in the desert for a spell, and while he pumped gas he made me sit behind his desk—where I could feel the fan. I spent an hour there, listening to this fellow and answering questions on what I'd seen. But I couldn't put it off forever. A relatively flat twenty-one miles to Green River—and the anti-climactic end of a thousand-mile loop—awaited me.

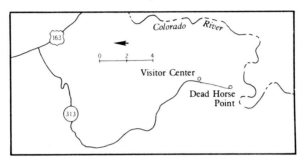

The only choice for going west is Interstate 70 for seven miles, but at **Floy Station** US 6 veers off into town. That night I slept in the public camp-ground on the south edge of town, and the next morning, while strolling to a cafe, met a very nice lady from Iowa walking her poodle. We stood next to the waters which helped carve what I had seen, down which Major Powell had travelled to immortality, and talked of her dog's operation. The loop was truly over.

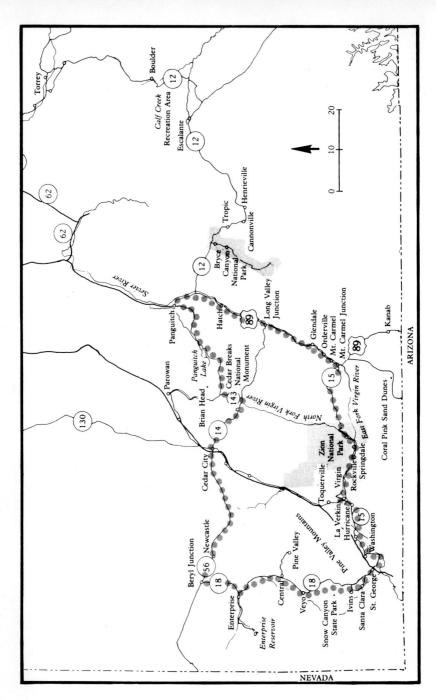

3. ZION LOOP

CEDAR CITY—CEDAR BREAKS—
PANGUITCH—MOUNT CARMEL JUNCTION—
ZION—ST. GEORGE—ENTERPRISE—
NEWCASTLE—CEDAR CITY

Mileage: 268

Spur A	BOULDER MONUMENT	176 miles (roundtrip)	
Spur B	BRYCE CANYON NATIONAL PARK	42 "	"
Spur C	CORAL PINK SAND DUNES STATE PARK	30 "	"
Spur D	ZION CANYON	12 "	"
Spur E	PINE VALLEY	22 "	"
Spur F	ENTERPRISE RESERVOIR	28 "	"

Mileage: 310

The spectacular beauty of this loop—of Zion and Bryce National Parks, and of Cedar Breaks National Monument—is difficult to imagine. And the beauty seems to be especially augmented with travelling through on a bike.

Think of a five-mile descent in Zion, a one-mile tunnel ride through rock, then towering thousand-foot cliffs and canyon walls above you. Or Bryce, whose brochure tells of "12 enormous amphitheaters plunging down a thousand feet through nearly 60 different colored layers of pink and white limestone." And dazzling color once again at Cedar Breaks, plus hundreds of formations of every conceivable shape.

Other loop attractions include Snow Canyon State Park, where black lava and red sand contrast brilliantly in sunlight, and Pine Valley, Utah's Swiss village in the hills. A petrified forest and Coral Pink Sand Dunes and roads of evergreen at ten thousand feet; all of this in a two-week ride of forty miles per day. Concerning distances, this loop is notable for the many route alternatives it offers. Due to the configurations of mountains and roads, it's possible to see much of the above in a trip of only 235 miles, or *one* week of pedalling forty miles per day. But there's a catch; you'd miss much of the history which the longer loop takes in.

If you choose to take the entire loop and all the spurs you'll meet some old friends of the trail—Dominguez and Escalante, and the Hole-in-the-Rock party. Another portion of the Old Spanish Trail is here also, plus the Southwest expedition of Jedediah Smith. Jacob Hamblin's home is on the loop, as well as Brigham Young's winter residence, and the picturesque ghost town of Grafton— immortalized by a bad-luck cyclist in the movie *Butch Cassidy and the Sundance Kid.* A site of great historical importance along Loop Three is the now-quiet field where the Mountain Meadows Massacre took place.

There are no very long stretches without water on this loop, and except for the spur to Boulder you'll never be more than three hours from a cafe. I've ridden this area on five different tours—in groups, by myself, and in all four seasons. The great altitude differences allow you to tailor a cool summer ride by sticking to the high country, or remain fairly warm in winter by touring the lower elevations in Utah's "Dixie."

Cedar City is an excellent place to begin the loop. If you're travelling from Salt Lake, plan a day for getting there (5½ hours driving time), finding somewhere to leave your car, and for seeing the city's sights. There's the Globe Theatre, home of the annual Shakespearean Festival on Southern Utah State College's lovely campus. The Iron Mission State Historical Monument, on the very northern end of Main Street, is a museum which houses many pioneer relics. Closer to downtown is the Old Rock Church, on the corner of Main and Center. You'll pass this grand old Mormon chapel as you head out toward Cedar Breaks; take time for one of the public tours.

When you're ready to tackle the mountains, return to the corner of Main and Central (next to Zions National Bank), and proceed east on Utah 14. A sign there says "Cedar Breaks 21—Summit ahead 10,000 feet." Don't let it get to you. After all, you're already at 5800'. And remember when you read the next sign (at MP 1—"8% grades next 40 miles. Turn around here") that *your* big pull is for only eighteen miles—*not* forty. I've done the climb three times and am still alive; it isn't nearly as bad as most people imagine.

The ride is made easier for another reason as well—the beautiful scenery. In only a few miles you run through red rock to gray, from juniper and cottonwood to pine and fir and quakies. I've done the climb twice in March, once in June. In early spring the water races down the canyon, cascading over rocks along the road for miles. In summer the flow is lessened, but wild-flowers sit in view on shaded forest floors. Birds are plentiful, and deer are often seen in morning and evening hours.

Two restaurants (steaks and seafood—open evenings) lie a few miles up the canyon; a waterfall at **MP 7+** is a great place for a rest. Near **MP 11** the road levels off momentarily, and in a half-mile more you reach the Woods Ranch Iron County Recreation Area—complete with barbecue pits and covered picnic tables. It's eighteen miles to the **Cedar Breaks National Monument** turnoff, but only the first fifteen are rough.

Head north on Utah 143 when you're at the top, after you've had your fill of the views to the southwest, and marvelled at the three-foot snowbanks which sit in shaded areas even in the month of June. You'll climb slightly in this pretty alpine setting for a mile and a half, then drop a bit to the Visitor Center/Park Headquarters. (There are campgrounds around, but be ready for night-time temperatures in the thirties even in summer. The *all-time* high for Cedar Breaks is only 80°!) The small park headquarters has exhibits of life zones and geologic history; afterwards, take a stroll to the edge of the cliff. If you're fortunate enough to have a bright sun, the view will leap at you. Orange-colored rock configurations stand in a giant bowl, sculpted by un-counted mountain showers.

The road continues north, winding through the forest and offering occasional views to the west. You'll climb for these few miles and then come to a junction. Straight ahead for two miles is **Brian Head** Ski Resort (motels, restaurants); turn right and you won't touch your pedals for the first three miles, and then enjoy an easy ride for another twelve to Panguitch Lake. This bright blue mountain lake turns jet black in a storm, which can come on suddenly at such an altitude. Lodging, campgrounds, cafes, and a grocery are here, plus pretty flowered meadows and long-needle pines. It's then fifteen miles of fast but gradual descents to **Panguitch** (motels, grocery, cafe).

SPURS A & B—BOULDER/BRYCE—(218 miles roundtrip)

After enjoying a meal in town, proceed south on US 89 for eight miles, then east on Utah 12. US 89 has a pretty steady flow of traffic, but it's also blessed with a four-foot-wide shoulder at this point. The pretty Sevier River runs alongside, assisting the many canyon washes in irrigating the green valley to the east.

Bryce Canyon National Park lies seventeen miles from the junction of 12 and 89, but the scenery begins almost immediately up this road. A sign proclaims "Red Canyon," and so it is. Seven miles of constant grade come before the summit of 7619' is reached, but the climb is so gradual in most places that it merely allows you longer gazes at the canyon walls. You'll pass campgrounds, motels, and restaurants in the first fourteen miles, and a grocery two miles before the turnoff on Utah 63 to the Park.

Head south on 63 for just over a mile and you'll come to Ruby's Inn—a giant motel complex with everything from horses to helicopter rides and HBO. Then comes the final two-mile pull into the Park. (It is uphill, I'm afraid, but not steep.) Campgrounds in Bryce are often full in summer (reserve one early in the day), and cabins require much earlier reservations. Contact TWA in Cedar City, the private concessionaire in Zion and Bryce, for information. But wherever you stay, give yourself time to walk around. In fact, if it's a choice between the fifteen-mile one-way ride to road's end at Rainbow Point, and an afternoon of short hikes in the maze of colorful formations—choose the walks. I've taken them in summer, and snowshoed the trails on Christmas Eve, and never lost the feeling of a gerbil in a splendid cage. (Pick up the free brochure on day hikes at the Visitor Center. There's also a restaurant at the Lodge.)

You'll not be sorry if you *do* take the ride, however, for wonderful views of these configurations also exist from above, as well as the opportunity to see for miles across the rugged land toward Boulder. The Park road narrows after the Lodge turnoff, but no trailers are allowed past that point. (Do watch out for those motorists who nevertheless continue to drive with their extremely wide "trailer-mirrors" attached.) Two or three miles after the Lodge you'll wince as you read the sign "Steep Grades—Sharp Curves—Next 14 Miles." But it isn't *all* up. Several level and even slightly downgrade sections are yours on the trip out to Rainbow Point (9095').

My ride from Bryce to Boulder is one of the most memorable days I've ever spent in the saddle. Planning to meet a friend of mine that afternoon at spur's end (and catch a ride back to the loop), I left most of my touring gear with him at his Park Ranger's residence. After all, what could possibly happen in seventy-five short miles? But it was a stupid and almost very costly mistake.

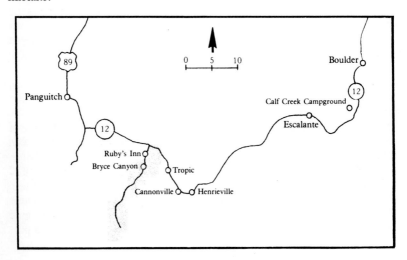

From the junction of State Hwys 12 and 63, where you earlier turned south for the Park, head east. The road surface is smooth, the terrain for the first thirteen miles (to a bit past Cannonville) is mostly downhill. There's an especially great descent to the town of **Tropic** (8 miles), which has a grocery, cafe, and also boasts the cabin of the man whose name was applied to the canyon and park you've just enjoyed—Ebenezer Bryce. (The cabin sits on the west side of the road as you head out of town toward Boulder.)

Cannonville comes only five miles after Tropic, and **Henrieville** three miles after that. (Don't count on food in either place.) Jackrabbits, cottontails, and birds abound in this watered area, and after Henrieville the cultivated fields give way to brown hills and gray formations. High sage and wildflowers contend with a wide assortment of trees and bushes for living space, and the Henrieville Creek runs along this slightly rolling road in a deep-walled chasm which it had carved before even the Anasazi came. A one-mile sharp climb begins at **MP 37+**, then a fast descent followed by a two-mile switchback climb through rock which made me think of the Dakota Badlands. I'd been baking in the heat from Tropic to Henrieville, but now the huge dark clouds which had been following behind me caught me at the mountain pass, and sent me scurrying for raingear as the first big, cold droplets hit my naked back. In a minute the real deluge began, and I crept back into the pine and juniper to escape it. I huddled there, becoming chilled, and wishing I'd brought my normal complement of foul-weather cycling gear. As it was I had only my poncho, and by day's end would feel like a human sponge.

At first the chill was pleasant, having been hot on so many summer rides. I sat on a large white rock, watching the rain perform its magic on the little space of red earth before me. It was on a small scale what I'd been riding through for weeks, and I could therefore easily imagine myself reduced a hundred times in size. The ground absorbed little of the rain, and soon the drops combined to form slender rivulets in the sand. These raced past and down the hill, carrying away the bits of pine cone I tossed out to gauge the water's strength and speed. I'd read somewhere that water moving at one foot per second can carry gravel in its wake, and at twenty-five feet per second can do the same with boulders. Then, as I crouched over the tiny newly formed stream, dropping bits of wood and measuring the distance travelled as I counted "One chimpanzee, two chimpanzee" (I didn't have my watch...), the rain turned into hail. Thus an abrupt and painful end to my attempt at scientific observation.

When the storm passed I jumped back in the saddle, and five miles west of Escalante came to the dirt paths leading north to nearby cliff dwellings. But the rain had made the roads impassable for my narrow touring tires. Three miles east of this is the turnoff to the Escalante Petrified Forest State Park. It's worth a visit, and has a pretty campground near a little lake to boot. Then the final two miles to the town of **Escalante (MP 60)**, and a huge chef's salad at its only restaurant. The place also has four motels, a campground and grocery, and many nineteenth-century buildings which are still in use.

From Escalante it's only twenty-four miles to Boulder, but these are the most scenic of the spur. About six miles east is the dirt road which the Hole-in-the-Rock party, after resupplying in Escalante, took south in 1879. (Though the townspeople told me it wasn't so, some of the "notchers" complained of un-Christian price-gouging. One pioneer later wrote in his autobiography, "The People of Escalante, on hearing of our coming, held a convention and raised the prices of everything we would be likely to need, almost double what it was before.")

At **MP 65** you'll begin two climbs which consume nearly five miles; then a sign will warn you of sharp curves and steep grades (9%) for the next two miles. Pay attention to the warning. They come on fast, and quickly take you from white and gray landscapes to red rock and water. I found it even prettier than Red Canyon, for the road twists through a narrow gorge, while water sculpts the slickrock on each side. And then comes another mountain pass, a rough one, one that tried to kill me.

For an hour a second storm had been rolling inexorably toward me, but taking its sweet time. Glancing behind now and then to judge its progress, I hoped it would drench me before the climb. I'd caught two marble-like hailstones on my nose that morning, and wanted to avoid getting beaned again. Concentrating on this possibility, I'd given little thought to the danger of strong winds in this high country.

I'd been in sculpted slickrock and narrow canyons for half an hour, and therefore hadn't noticed that the wind was blowing hard. Admiring the Calf Creek Campground about two hundred feet below the road, I pedalled around a cliff face on this mountain climb, and into a wall of wind.

It happened with lightning speed. The giant gust caught my front panniers and handlebar bag (my rear saddlebags were back at Bryce), and whipped the front wheel around. I was thrown by this tremendous wind toward the road's edge—and the drop-off to the gorge. Finally my mind caught up with what was happening, and, unable to control the direction of the bike, I pulled down on the left side of the handlebars with all my strength. Like a cowboy wrestling a steer to the ground, but *feeling* like the steer, I brought the bike and me to a stop with still six feet to spare. Had there been any traffic I would have been hit—if not at first when the wind tossed me across the lane—then as I lay in the road wrapped around my bike. I hadn't acted until the edge was almost too near, and that terrifying view of the gorge was more real in my eyes than what I was actually seeing.

A long half-minute passed before I rose. Lifting my bike, I found that I'd wrenched by left shoulder either in the effort to stop, or in the fall itself. I nursed it to the mountain pass, while quieting my nerves. The rain began, but I still walked my bike, leaning into winds which brought to mind the Santa Fe Trail in Kansas—when I was literally blown *out* of the saddle.

Thunder and lightning began, with brilliant bolts lighting up that land of rounded surfaces. A million years of storms like this had molded sandstone into slickrock. Near the top a crack of lightning came so close that I thought it wise to separate myself from metal. I laid my bike down on the rocks and walked a hundred feet away. Choosing a pine much shorter than most around, I nestled into it for what protection it could give.

Ten miles and two cold, wet hours later, I stood in a small market in **Boulder**. A fellow had driven in a half-hour after me, asking if there was a motel around. (There is—the Circle Cliffs—but it was full of folks waiting out the weather.) "I'll sleep anywhere," he said, "but I don't want to face that road again in this storm!" He was out of luck. No vacancy, no cafe, and no paved road in any direction except back to Bryce.

(Don't miss the eleventh-century Anasazi Indian village and museum in Boulder, and if you're on a mountain bike the thirty-six-mile dirt road—up and over 11,000' Boulder Mountain—to Torrey is a must. But—go prepared!)

The mountain biker won't be happy, but thin-tire cyclists will love the news: the road from Boulder north to Utah 24 is now paved. Look at the map and you'll see that this development puts Capitol Reef National Park into reach—if you're willing to add the miles. The route is beautiful, the climb a bit of a challenge.

One development all cyclists will like however, is that Boulder now boasts a cafe, open from late spring to early fall.

Back to the loop at last—at the junction of US 89 and Utah 12. The nine-mile ride from the junction south to **Hatch** (motels, cafe) is very much like the pretty stretch from Panguitch, with a wide shoulder and relatively level ground. The thirteen miles after that to **Long Valley Junction** has a couple of good hills; the Sevier River runs alongside, plus the attractive western face of the Paunsaugunt Plateau. At Long Valley (just before **MP 104**), Utah 14 heads up for twenty-two pretty miles to Cedar Breaks, offering the cyclist with little time the opportunity to make a quick return.

It's a good, long descent to Glendale fourteen miles south. The east fork of the Virgin River cups the road, and you follow her through narrow canyon walls at the end of the run. Halfway to Glendale the evergreens begin, and though there's been no wide shoulder since Long Valley, in most places enough remains to move right when traffic forces you. (A KOA sits in a pretty spot four miles before the town.)

Glendale comes at **MP 90+**, and has an old restored hotel (Smith's) and grocery store. It's then three miles more to Orderville (motel, grocery, cafe), a town so named because the residents for a dozen years lived as a Mormon "United Order" co-operative, at the behest of Brigham Young. Five miles of easy pedalling (near **MP 82**) then brings you to **Mount Carmel Junction** (motel, cafe). From there it's up the hill and then down into Zion National Park on Utah 9, or south to the brilliantly colored Coral Pink Sand Dunes Stake Park. (Utah 15 has been recenty changed to Utah 9 on some road signs and more recent highway maps. Consider the two interchangeable.)

SPUR C—CORAL PINK SAND DUNES—(30 miles roundtrip)

The first four miles of this spur are on US 89—and almost completely uphill. Take your mind off the climb by concentrating on the majestic peaks of the Elkhart Cliffs. I've seen them twice in winter, and love how fog will curl around their waists, while the snow-topped peaks stand free to catch the sun. A two-lane paved road strikes south from US 89 for thirteen slightly downhill miles to beautiful campgrounds at the Dunes. Pink sand and evergreen mixed with sage are yours to enjoy on this ride.

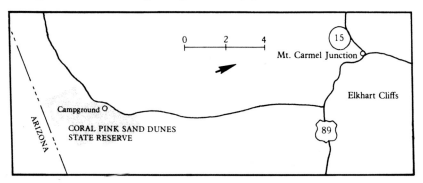

The road from Mount Carmel Junction to Zion Park begins with a bear of a climb; but you're rewarded near the top with another view of the Elkhart Cliffs. **MP 56** comes halfway up this hill, and you'll have rolling terrain and pretty countryside all the way to the East Zion Indian Store at **MP 47** (snacks and soda, and the Park entrance nearby). From here you begin to catch glimpses of what is in my opinion the most spectacular of all Utah's park areas. The Virgin River has worked for millions of years to create the marvelous steep-walled and many-colored canyons, cutting into the earth like a knife held in place as the huge plateau rose from sea level to an altitude of several thousand feet around it. Like the tiny rivulets of rainwater carving their paths in sand on the ride to Boulder, this crashing river, swollen by storms and melting snow, has worn away so much rock that much of what can be seen is Navajo sandstone, laid down 160 million years ago.

It is by far best to enter **Zion National Park** from the east. The entrance elevation there is 5700', the Visitor Center near the west entrance is only 4000'. Not only is this easier on the legs, but it provides spectacular first views of the canyons down below. But be careful! The roads are narrow, as in most parks, and motorists (like cyclists) are craning necks to see the *sights,* not traffic.

You have two tunnels in the first four miles—a very short one which presents little difficulty, and a second one that is dangerous, more than a mile long, and off-limits to cyclists without a motor escort. (It is very dark inside, raising the possibility of an accident.) On my last visit I was told to wait at the mouth of the tunnel and flag down a car, then ask the driver to turn on his lights and drive very slowly behind me until I had reached the other side.

Years ago one was to call the park headquarters (801-772-3256) for a ranger escort, but that proved too time-consuming due to the number of cyclists. Bikers were also allowed to proceed by themselves if equipped with lights, but this too has changed. Be sure to check at the entrance station (or call ahead) for current tunnel passage requirements.

SPUR D—ZION CANYON—(12 miles roundtrip)

Your view, once on the other side and back in sunlight, is fabulous. And so is your descent through switchbacks to the canyon floor. At the bottom you'll come to a paved road angling north; take it. This twelve-mile roundtrip spur is, for the investment, the most worthwhile in the state. You'll pedal an almost level road up this canyon created by the north fork of the Virgin River. Halfway up is the Zion Lodge (closed in winter) which has rooms, a restaurant, and horseback riding for those who aren't yet tired of being in the saddle. Again, the lodge and other concessions with the Park are operated by TWA. Contact them in Cedar City for reservations. Past the Lodge the road curves around the river, next to sheer sandstone faces which rise 1500'. At the road's end is the green and scenic mile-long "Gateway to the Narrows" walk. And here, as in Bryce, you'll not regret the time you spend hiking. (Free pamphlets of all the trails are available at the Visitor Center.)

After returning to the main canyon road it's only a mile or so south to the Visitor Center, and one-third of a mile beyond that to the first of two campgrounds in the Park. (The second is another quarter-mile south, almost at the Park's west entrance.) A mile and a half outside the boundary is the town of **Springdale**, with a grocery, restaurants, motels, and a campground with hot showers available (for a small fee) even to those staying elsewhere.

Four miles south of Springdale is the town of **Rockville** (no services). Two of its buildings—the post office and Deseret Telegraph—were erected at the time of the Civil War. It also has an old bridge which must be crossed to see Utah's most picturesque ghost town—**Grafton**. At this writing a three-and-a-half-mile dirt road heads off to the cemetery and town, but access may soon be made much easier; a developer has purchased it and plans to conduct public tours.

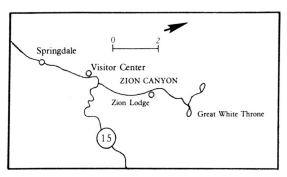

The ride from the Park is excellent. It parallels the river and is downhill almost all the way to Virgin (snacks and soda) near **MP 19**. This is an area of immense geologic features and much greenery, and becomes even more verdant as you approach St. George. The road is narrow and on summer days carries a great deal of traffic, but two miles west of Virgin a new wide-shouldered highway surface begins. A few good climbs and then it's a long, fast descent to Utah 17 (one-half mile past **MP 13**). A KOA sits at this junction; a drive-in is just south. (See Chapter Nine for a route due north from here to Cedar City.)

Before we get too far away from Virgin, let me offer yet another route option. As you enter that little town you will see a sign for Kolob Road. Make a right if your legs and lungs are up for a tough climb and your eyes ready for sage, yellow grass, oak brush brilliant in fall, black lava, swirling slickrock patches, and strange cone-shaped mountains in the distance. The pavement ends after fifteen miles or so, and your return to the loop will be a great downhill run.

Four miles south on Hwy 17 is the town of **Hurricane** (motels, grocery, cafe, campground); on the way you'll cross the wide Virgin River gorge, then climb a hill which sports a sign for the nearby Pah Tempe Hot Springs. In 1776 the Dominguez and Escalante expedition came very close to this spot. They had been travelling south along the Hurricane Cliffs in October, and found the going rough: "We halted near the valley's southern pass, without water for ourselves and for the horse herd. Tonight we were in direst need, with nothing by way of food, and so we decided to deprive a horse of its life so as not to forfeit our own...." (The *only* advantage of equestrianism over biking!)

Jedediah Smith, fur trapper and explorer, came through this region in the fall of 1826. But where the padres crossed the Virgin and fought the dry and mountainous terrain back to Santa Fe, Smith and his party followed the river's deep gorge south of St. George, to its junction with the Colorado. There they rested and then travelled west for sixteen days, across the desert to the San Bernadino Valley—the first white men to reach California overland.

You'll enjoy a long descent after Hurricane, then pay for it with a two-mile climb. From the summit, looking south and west, you'll have a panoramic view of what the two-hundred-mile-long Hurricane Fault, the Virgin River, volcanoes, and erosion have done to this land. The colored uplifts and shadowed steep declines are outstanding, even to an eye yet dazzled by the geology of Zion.

Okay. You've got a choice to make. The easiest and fastest way to St. George, after the nine-mile ride from Hurricane to I-15, is to jump on Interstate 15 for seven miles to the first exit. (*Not* the Middleton exit, unless you want to do some steep climbing to St. George.) But a far more preferable route is the easy-to-ride, difficult-to-follow path through Washington. Twice the distance of the interstate, the ride is worth every extra minute. Let me try to make it understandable.

Just west of **MP 1** (one mile east of I-15, near Harrisburg Junction) you'll see a sign for the local sanitary landfill. It's an inauspicious beginning, but you'll never see the dump. Follow this sign off Utah 9 to an unnamed Washington County road heading south, down a long hill, past the landfill turnoff, then up a steep climb. From the top you can see the town of Washington ahead, plus the traffic on the interstate. Race down this hill another couple of miles and you'll be in **Washington**. The town has a motel, restaurant, and an 1860s cotton mill, but all this comes a few blocks past your turnoff left on 300 East Street. Make your turn, and head south out of town.

Ride through country smells and hay fields, continuing south through two intersections, across an irrigation ditch to a sign which shows an arrow pointing right. Another sign says "Warner Valley 3 Miles" to the left. Follow the main road and the arrow to the right. During the next two miles or so you'll have several sideroads coming in; remain on the main road which angles south or west. You'll strike the Virgin once again; follow it due west (you can see from here the huge letter "D" painted on the hillside above St. George—for "Dixie College"), until you see a yield sign at the bridge. Make a right and cross the river. The road heads north past the first intersection, turns west slightly, then takes a sharp turn left to head under I-15 and into **St. George**. You've entered the city on 700 South Street; the first intersection is 700 East. Make a right so as to be heading north on 700 East, and it will take you to the main drag of St. George Boulevard at the Four Seasons Convention Center.

St. George is remarkable. Its altitude of only 2880' is a half-mile lower than Cedar City (only fifty-three miles to the north). The cyclist can view plants and flowers here which are seen nowhere else in the state. But to enjoy this town you'll have to get off St. George Boulevard, home of motels and fast food outlets, and even faster cars and trucks. The tourists own the road by day, the local teenagers take over at night. (Of the two, the kids are safer drivers; at least they *know* where they're going.) Take in Brigham Young's winter home a block north of this boulevard (and 100 West), and then tour the downtown area further south. The Tabernacle has public tours, and the Temple grounds are refreshingly green.

Once you've seen the city, proceed west on St. George Boulevard until it dead-ends at Utah 18. Make a right and travel north for 1½ miles, to signs which indicate "left to Santa Clara," "straight ahead to Snow Canyon." On my initial ride in this area I followed the sign to Snow Canyon due north, and sorely regretted it. Not only is the road one tough climb until MP 7 (about 5½ miles), but you then drop down nearly a thousand feet into the Park, and climb out again to continue the loop.

Instead, make a left at the sign for Santa Clara, and head west to this bucolic former colony of Swiss LDS converts. The road is named Sunset Boulevard, and once again you can see wondrous depressions, uplifts, peaks and ridges out ahead. **Santa Clara** has a grocery, and just west of its shaded streets is Jacob Hamblin's home. Take time to tour this two-story house, for you'll see not only the home, but many implements with which late nineteenth-century people accomplished household chores. (You'll find the older

Mormon missionaries who conduct such tours extremely patient—both in explanations of looms and rope-beds, and in answering the recurrent questions about polygamy.)

One mile west, past the Indian missionary's home (Hamblin spent the greater part of his life in this peaceful pursuit), is a sign pointing north to Snow Canyon and the tiny community of **Ivins**. Make a right on this county road and travel north past "The Pantry" (groceries and snacks) to the first major road heading east. There is a sign (low and easy to miss on the right side) just before this intersection which shows Snow Canyon to the right. Take the road and proceed east past Padre Estates(!) to the first road heading north (no sign here). Some state maps indicate this is dirt, though it's pavement all the way—a mile or so—to **Snow Canyon State Park,** and then through it for three miles and up the giant hill back to Utah 18.

What a sandbox! For scrambling, camping, and just lying in the shade, the place is great. Volcanic rock and red sand set off the park in colors which dazzle the eyes, especially beneath the azure skies of southern Utah. On my first visit there—when I'd made the mistake of coming due north from St. George—I spent the afternoon in conversation with four couples from Las Vegas. All retired, they sat like happy lizards in the sun, enjoying the out-of-doors and going, now and then, inside their Winnebagos for cold beer. We whiled away the hottest hours in pleasant conversation, as I listened to stories of the Depression and World War II, of children's careers and happy times. Then, filled with cold liquids and warm memories, I headed north toward the infamous site of the Mountain Meadows massacre.

The road after Snow Canyon is much easier, with minor dips and climbs, and extinct volcanoes and Spanish bayonet to look at. Juniper and sage return in force, and then give way to cultivated fields in **Dameron Valley** (cafe and food at the "Mercantile"). It's a mile upgrade past the store, then a great descent before a slight uphill pull to Veyo (grocery), which sits on the banks of the Santa Clara River, and also on the northward bend of the Old Spanish Trail.

SPUR E—PINE VALLEY—(22 miles roundtrip)

Six relatively easy miles from Veyo lies the turnoff for **Pine Valley** (the road is unnamed, but a sign is present; it's seven miles east to the town—another four to the campground). I took it late in the day, with the sun fading as quickly as my energy. Fifteen-foot-high cliffrose, solid tree-covered hillsides, deep rock chasms made by the Santa Clara, and a herd of free-grazing cows all greeted me. And then came the last hill of the day, which allowed me to look down on the village lying at nearly seven thousand feet, nestled into mountains whose peaks soar a half-mile higher still.

The following morning I had the most enjoyable breakfast of the entire tour. I'd pedaled back into town from the campground, past high country greenery and a mountain lake, and a half-dozen deer who eyed me as I rode past. I stopped at the Brandin' Iron Steakhouse (on the only road in town; no motel, very small grocery), hoping merely to warm my chilled hands around a cup of coffee, and eat a plate of cakes. But then I met Gary and Dorothy, who were opening the place that morning. It was nearly noon when I tore myself from their fine food and splendid conversation, from stories of John D. Lee and tips on raising rabbits, to begin my ride.

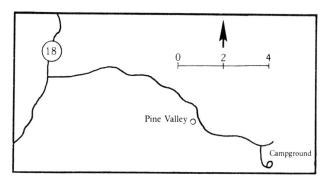

I didn't get very far. The Mormon church in town was built by our old friend whose cabin we visited on the way to Boulder, Ebenezer Bryce. The tour brought on another spate of conversation with the missionary guide. And then I spent an unplanned hour in the Pine Valley cemetery.

I often visit graveyards in small towns. Reading dates, trying to put together family names, the imagination conjures vivid scenes of local history. But what I found here surprised me. Most of us have read statistics on infant mortality. But the names, dates and verses on these tombstones brought the facts into sadly sharpened focus.

A little time on earth he spent,
Till God for him his angels sent.

That couplet on a marker for a child who died in 1899, a month after birth. Next to it:

A precious one from us has gone
A voice we loved is stilled,
A place is vacant in our hearts
Which never can be filled.

Same parents. This child had died at five.

And more. So many more children. Beyond remorse, some verses told the role religion played in easing the sorrow, and ascribing the loss to some great but murky cause.

Other surprises were contained in the biographies detailed there. This town, whose pine lumber was used in scores of early settlements in the desert areas of Utah and Nevada, whose wood contained the right degree of resin for use in the Salt Lake Tabernacle organ, likewise spread her people wide around the world. One spent ten years as a missionary with the Maoris in New Zealand. Another marched with the Mormon Battalion against Mexico. A third, a young lieutenant, was missing in action in France a week after D-Day.

I pedalled north on Utah 18 once again, over very rough terrain. But this was still the easiest route through the mountains, the route taken by early Indians, the Spanish, the California-bound emigrants, and by today's motorists. Recalling stories I'd heard at breakfast, I toiled up the hills with my mind on others than myself. Such as the hundred-odd Chinese, who a century ago labored for the railroad only a mountain away from Pine Valley. Or Gary's mother, who'd shot and killed the huge stretched cougar on the Brandin' Iron wall. But most of all, and then to the exclusion of all else as I neared the spot, my thoughts stayed on the Mountain Meadows Massacre.

It was September of 1857. The Mormons had been busy in their State of Deseret for a full decade; Brigham Young's colonization program had stretched the church-linked borders in all directions. Parowan and Cedar City had recently been established, and lived tenuously among much larger Indian populations. And then, while celebrating the tenth anniversary of their July 24th arrival in the Salt Lake Valley at the top of Big Cottonwood Canyon, messengers appeared from the east. Their words were chilling, especially to a people who had tasted blood before. An army was marching upon them, a United States army, sent by the president to "put down the rebellion."

It would take too long to discuss the reasons for this expedition. Let me merely suggest that the Mormons, having suffered persecution everywhere they'd been, and having lost hundreds of lives in the move west (to a spot which was, when they first arrived, *not* U.S. territory), had not welcomed the national government's civil officers with open arms. It could be called the Utah Territory, but to the Mormons it was still the theocratic State of Deseret.

Nevertheless, the people were astounded at the news, for there was no rebellion. And there would be no retreat, nor any further movement west. Not this time.

Brigham Young's plan went out: "Waylay our enemies, attack them from ambush, stampede their animals, take the Supply trains . . . .To waste away our enemies and lose none. . ."

The invading army was led by General Albert Sidney Johnston, a man who four years later was to fight against the Union as a Confederate officer, and bleed to death at the battle of Shiloh. His welcome was prepared. Mormons burned Fort Bridger, and manned the mountaintops in Echo Canyon. Word went out to all—make ready for a long winter siege, cache food and supplies in the hills, be prepared to set fire to all you've worked so hard to build. Like the Russians against Napoleon, nothing of use to the enemy was to be left untorched.

Into this maelstrom came an emigrant wagon train. Everything, it seemed, conspired to seal its fate as the only real casualty of the "Mormon War." It was the first to take the route through southern Utah after word of the approaching army had reached those settlements. It was composed of some who antagonized the Mormons, by naming their oxen after church leaders and cursing them loudly while travelling through towns. Some members of this "Fancher Party" wagon train came from Arkansas and Missouri, and inspired ugly memories of early days. (Some southern Utah residents had been wounded at Haun's Mill,

Missouri, in 1838. The atrocity took place when more than two hundred militiamen attacked a settlement of thirty Mormon families. Seventeen people died outright, including a wounded old man who was executed, and a small boy who, when captured, was shot through the head.)

The emigrants also enticed the local Indians with their well-stocked wagons and prime cattle herd. When some Mormon towns refused to sell them supplies, the emigrants boasted that once in California they'd raise an army and return. This threat seemed all too real to a people who had one force already bearing down on them, and had been forewarned to be on the lookout for a second army which might come overland from the west coast. Finally, word came that church leader (and road builder—Loop One), Parley Pratt had been stabbed to death—in Arkansas.

The result of these component parts to tragedy—the actual battle and final massacre scene—would require several grisly pages to relate. On the site a marker reads:

Mountain Meadows—A favorite recruiting place on the Old Spanish Trail— In this vicinity, September 7-11, 1857, occurred one of the most lamentable tragedies in the annals of the West. A company of about 140 Arkansas and Missouri emigrants led by Captain Charles Fancher, enroute to California, was attacked by white men and Indians. All but seventeen, being small children, were killed. John D. Lee, who confessed participation as leader, was legally executed here March 23, 1877. Most of the emigrants were buried in their own defense pits. This monument was reverently dedicated September 10, 1932, by the Utah Pioneer Trails and Landmarks Association and the people of southern Utah.

It is now believed the total number killed was closer to one hundred, and that while the seventeen children referred to were sent back to families in the East, an eighteenth child remained in Utah, grew up as a Mormon, and married a man of that church. Brigham Young, who had been informed of the Fancher Party threats, had sent a rider to the area with orders to let them pass. Obviously, with a Gentile army approaching Utah, and still hoping for a peaceful settlement to the entire misconceived "war" (which is in fact what finally took place—thanks to an early winter storm which stopped the Union force in Wyoming), a massacre by Mormons would be a great mistake. But the messenger arrived as Cedar City residents were burying the dead.

Three miles or so north of the Pine Valley turnoff is the sign for the massacre site, though it says merely "Mountain Meadow." A one-mile rough dirt road leads west, ending at the creek from which the Fancher train drew water during those long days of desperate struggle. You'll have to park your bike and walk the path across the stream, then up into the meadow where it took place. So peaceful now; perhaps a quote by Jacob Hamblin—who visited the site a week after the massacre—will help you imagine that more troubled time.

I went to the place of slaughter! Where those unfortunate people were slain. Oh! horrible, indeed was the sight—language fails to picture the scene of blood and carnage . . . . At three places the wolves had disinterred the bodies and stripped the bones of their flesh, had left them strewed in every direction.

It took a while to free myself of thoughts about the massacre, but in another fifteen miles of relatively easy riding I reached **Enterprise** (cafe— closed when I was there—grocery, but no motel), turned left into town, and treated myself to a quart of chocolate milk at the general store. The world was suddenly much brighter.

SPUR F—ENTERPRISE RESERVOIR—(28 miles roundtrip)

Six miles of flat riding along Shoal Creek, west of Enterprise, puts you just beyond the steep northern extension of 7300′ Flat Top Mountain. Make a left at the junction and climb slightly to Enterprise Reservoir. Two campgrounds lie in this vicinity, but you'll have to hike about a mile to see the Honey Comb Rocks.

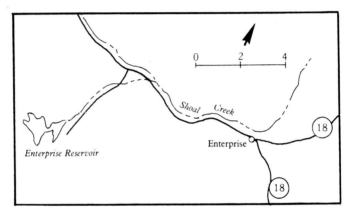

Now you're almost home. The eleven miles of pancake-flat riding from Enterprise north to **Beryl Junction** (Utah Hwys 18 and 56) are beautiful in spots. After the sadness of the Pine Valley cemetery and the massacre site, it was good to see cultivated fields, and hear meadowlarks as I passed. Woody's Cafe sits at the junction, and as you head east on 56 you'll pass a small gas-and-grocery after half a mile. A couple of minor hills in the six miles east to **Newcastle** (small market), then a four- or five-mile slight grade up—past a historical marker for a blacksmith shop on the Old Spanish Trail. Sage along the road, junipers to the side, barren, undulating country out ahead.

A bit more climbing is required near the gravel access road to the Iron-town ruins, and when high enough I stopped to gather pine gum from the trees. Then comes a very long descent of six or seven miles, through the red rocks of Leach Canyon and onto the Cedar Valley flats. In the distance I could make out the city, and the traffic on Interstate 15. Ten easy miles of pedalling ends this mountain loop.

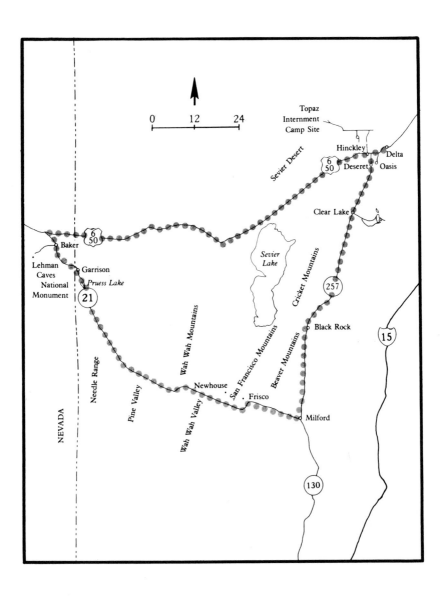

4. WESTERN DESERT LOOP

DELTA—MILFORD—BAKER (NEVADA)— DELTA

Mileage: 260

Spur A LEHMAN CAVES   12 miles (roundtrip)

Loop Four is tailor-made for those cyclists who like long rides with little traffic. In all of Utah, this is one of the most desolate areas—one leg of this triangular loop has a stretch of eighty-three miles without water, ninety-seven without services. I rode the Delta-to-Milford leg in January, while on a desert winter run from Salt Lake to Cedar City. Two years later I took the rest of the loop—in late June. With those experiences in mind, I suggest fall or spring for the ride, and then only if you're well equipped.

I know that some of you strong-legged, deep-lunged folks are going to see in this loop a perfect three-day ride. Well, it can be, but you'll miss a great deal of what it has to offer. The great vistas of the Wah Wah, San Francisco, and Confusion Mountains are in sight for tens of miles, as is the shimmering white surface of Sevier Dry Lake, and valleys which require two hours to cross. All these you'll experience even if you never leave the saddle.

But what you'll miss if you hurry through is the opportunity to visit a fort built in 1865, and an abandoned mining town which once housed six thousand people and twenty-three saloons. The single spur takes in a great cave tour, and if you add to it a few miles and an afternoon you can pedal up the highest mountain in Nevada, then hike the year-round ice field to the top. Dominguez and Escalante are once again with us, and we'll pedal near the site of later and less pleasant history—the Japanese-American Internment Camp at Topaz.

This loop does not offer excellent places to camp between the towns, however. If you dislike dry camping (no water at the site, beyond what you bring yourself), you'll have to pedal an entire leg each day. But, if you spend an extra twenty-four hours at Milford and Baker you'll see the attractions and be able to rest up a bit between long rides.

There are some rough climbs, but not many, and if you're fortunate in avoiding head winds you'll find this loop much easier than the first three. Though it seems strange in this desert region, be sure to inquire about road conditions west of Delta if the rains have been heavy; this stretch was under water for much of the spring of 1983.

The town of **Delta** has several motels, cafes and food stores, plus a central park area which exhibits a pioneer cabin and historical markers. One concerning nearby Topaz reads:

1942-1946 ... Fifteen miles west at Abraham is the location of the bleak desert site of a concentration camp, one of ten in western America, in which 110,000 persons of Japanese ancestry were interned against their will in World War Two. They were the victims of wartime hysteria, racial animosity, and economic opportunism on the West Coast. Confined behind barbed wire fences and guarded by armed sentries and held for no justifiable reason, the internees, two-thirds of whom were women and children, not only endured the bitter physical discomforts of the desert heat and cold, but sustained a shocking affront to their sense of justice and fair play and human dignity. May this grim episode of basic American principles gone astray remind us to work for understanding and good will, justice and an enlightened America today.

The former residents of Topaz remember with grateful appreciation the friendliness and understanding with which the people of Delta received us during the period of our trial and despair.

It is possible to visit the actual site of this camp, though there is little remaining but a few cement foundations thickly overgrown with weeds. It lies at the end of a very confusing series of turns in a road maze north of Hinckley, and requires some pedalling on dirt. My suggestion is to read about it, recall that "wartime hysteria" and fear also caused the Mountain Meadows Massacre and a thousand other deplorable incidents throughout history, and pedal on toward Milford.

At the west end of Delta, on Main Street, is a viaduct. Ride over it and continue on this highway (US 6/50) as it curves south, then back west. After five miles you'll come to a sign which points south to Deseret (3 miles) and Milford (70 miles). Turn south here on Utah 257 and travel along the flat terrain to the attractive (but no services) town of Deseret. At the south end of this small settlement is a sign which says "No Services Next 67 Miles." Check your saddlebags for supplies, top off your water bottles, swallow hard, and head out.

But not too fast. For just a bit beyond the sign is **Fort Deseret**, or rather the few remaining walls of this 1865 structure. A marker explains that it was erected in just eighteen days, to assist nearby settlers in defending themselves during the Black Hawk War. In many places around the state markers tell of settlements (twenty-five in all) abandoned during this four-year struggle. The war came about when a group of three hundred or so warriors refused to move to reservations and, under the leadership of Black Hawk, began a guerilla campaign against the Mormons.

A few miles south of the fort is a dirt road leading west to another massacre site (though of lesser scale) where Captain John Gunnison and his seven member party were killed in October 1853 by the Pahvant Indians who were avenging the death of one of their tribe, but the government surveying party was not to blame. The town of Gunnison is named for this man.

My notes from the winter ride along this level stretch of road speak of great expanses of scrub desert, and the Cricket Mountains standing black against a gray January sky. (My friend and I had stocked up with provisions in Delta, so that in case a blizzard caught us before Milford we could at least eat until it passed.) The Union Pacific Railroad runs alongside Utah 257 almost all the way to Milford, and we stopped once for water at a small group of houses next to the tracks. I recall large flocks of sheep tended by men on horseback, fast, never-resting dogs, and sage and juniper covered with frost. The south wind was biting cold on exposed cheeks, but the pedalling kept me warm inside. (Don't get excited when you see Black Rock on the map—it isn't a town. Just a lime plant, but good for water in a pinch. Also, mileposts on this run end with 1 just before Milford.)

No matter the time of year, you'll be pleased to reach the little town of **Milford**. It has a hotel on Main Street, an IGA grocery (be sure to try the doughnuts sold there, made by Father Valene), the Hong Kong Cafe, a lovely train station, and a very interesting Heritage Park (located one block west of the Chevron Station, across the street from a motel.)

One of the many markers in Heritage Park speaks of the difficulties encountered by Dominguez and Escalante as they travelled south along almost the same route you've just ridden from Delta. Note the remarks on the Great Basin and the enormous, ancient Lake Bonneville; you'll encounter other markers and physical evidence of these elsewhere in the state.

As Dominguez and Escalante made their way south from Utah Valley, the nature of the land played a significant role in the fate of the expedition. Their course followed the eastern edge of the Great Basin, a geographic region between the Wasatch and Sierra Nevada Mountains, in which there is no outlet to the sea. During the Ice Age Milford was covered by a southern extension of Lake Bonneville. Today the shoreline of the ancient lake is visible on the nearby mountain slopes. However, the Great Salt Lake is all that remains of the 145 mile wide and 346 mile long lake which covered most of western and central Utah, parts of Nevada and Idaho. Thousands of years before Lake Bonneville, the mountains surrounding Milford were created by block faulting. It was the Beaver, Cricket, and Wah Wah ranges that presented the immediate obstacle to Dominguez and Escalante as they sought a route west toward Monterey. The deserts through which they passed reduced their supplies critically as the greasewood, sagebrush, and meager grass were an unsatisfactory source of food.... The scarcity of water in the desert caused delays, especially as horses wandered from camp in search of water. When moisture finally fell during the first week of October, it was in the form of snow, as the high altitude (5000 feet above sea level) brought freezing cold to the expedition.

You'll have to climb the high hill west of Main Street to leave town on Utah 21—past the big Catholic church, and the Last Chance Cafe. (The name is appropriate, if unoriginal.) Pack your own grub, for it's seventy-five miles to the next store, eighty-three to a cafe. A Catholic church in Utah is usually evidence of an economic base other than agriculture. While Brigham Young counseled his people not to forego the land for mining, thousands of Gentiles of the millions pouring into the United States in the late nineteenth century travelled to Utah to mine, and to work on the railroad. The large train station in Milford, and old Frisco mining town fifteen miles west, are evidence of this region's past.

The ride to the San Francisco Mountains is a long, gentle climb, and you'll enjoy visiting the town of **Frisco** before taking on the next three valleys—which constitute the remaining sixty miles to Garrison. A dirt road leads north for a short distance to the abandoned settlement, where remains of twenty-three saloons and houses for six thousand people stand mute in the wind. A school and a weekly paper gave this wild place a certain respectability, though not as much as the staid mining town of **Newhouse**, just around the mountain pass and west on Utah 21 for five miles, then north two miles on a dirt road. A dance hall and opera house were built there, but saloons were not allowed. (Mileposts begin at 75 outside of Milford; at **MP 62**—near Frisco—is a shaded picnic table next to the road.)

Once you've rounded the San Francisco Mountains you'll see the wide Wah Wah Range. (A friend suggested these dry crags should be called instead the *no* "wah-wahs.") I began the downhill run a bit before MP 62, and looking across to my next mountain pass guessed the distance at nine miles. I was off by almost twice that. Such errors in judgment in arid climates are today mere curiosities. Not so long ago, in the case of the Donner Party (whom we'll meet on Loop Seven), it meant death.

These are beautifully scenic miles. Sage and yellow-headed rabbitbrush, shadscale and tumbleweed grow in the valleys, and junipers dot the low mountain passes. But it was the interplay of sun and shadow across the grand valleys, the movement in minutes of dark and light patches across distances I required two hours to traverse, which constantly intrigued me.

At **MP 52**—downhill for nine miles, level for one—is a collection of buildings a half-mile north of the highway. I topped off my water bottles at this ranch, then proceeded west again up a surprisingly difficult grade to the summit at **MP 45**. Seventeen miles across the valley!

If you travel these western trails in summer you'll probably see whirlwinds, or dust devils, twisting madly over the desert floor. These generally harmless, entertaining sights are caused by extremely heated areas of the ground, which force columns of air above them to rise rapidly. When this happens, the cooler air alongside the column rushes in, twirling the dust particles made airborne by the uplifts.

You'll also kick up jack rabbits on your ride, and marvel at how fast they move once your bike's clicking sound has scared them into action. These inelegant nocturnal creatures are beautifully adapted to the environment. They radiate heat away from their bodies through huge, thin, well-veined ears, and are able to survive on water contained in vegetation alone. In winter these veins contract, and the ears are pressed down in the fur—except when cocked for sound.

You'll probably see pronghorns also, especially on the ride from Baker to Delta. Biologists contend that these are incorrectly called antelope (just as there is no true American "buffalo"), and that they, too, are well adapted to this region of extremes. The pronghorn's hairs are like insulating fibers of new sleeping bags—tubular in shape, with large air pockets inside. Lying flat next to the body, these follicles insulate nicely; in summer, while releasing body heat, they stand almost erect—the heat escaping between them.

Pine Valley, the second of these huge basins, is escaped at **MP 26**. It's a rough climb, but nothing like the first one. I'd watched a mountain storm gathering for over an hour, then move away before I got to it. The map will show that you're entering the south end of Snake Valley (speaking of which, I *did* see a couple of dead rattlers on this ride; watch for them, especially in old mining town buildings). You'll be going downhill or across level ground from the summit of **MP 26** to **MP 10**, and then climb slightly. The Burbank Hills to the north are great to study as you pedal by, block-faulting having tilted up huge pieces of earth, exposing the varied colors and thicknesses of rock layers. To the south lies the Needle Range, well named for the jagged points which are snow-capped even in early summer.

At the end of such a dry day's riding I could smell the water of **Pruess Lake** long before it came into view. Two old houses appear first, one of the same era as Frisco, the second a cabin from even earlier days. Then comes tall, luxuriant green grass, up to the bellies of the fat cows grazing in it. Finally, you see the lake itself, so inviting after lifeless dust and rock. I straddled my bike for some time, watching insects fly about above the water, then dive to lightly touch the surface, and return. All wind had ceased in the late twilight, and I wondered if the bugs were merely exalting in how big a ripple they could cause in the glass-like surface of the lake. Closer to the bank, scores of whirligigs sped about in circles, and birds watched patiently.

It's downhill for the three and a half miles to the town of **Garrison**. I passed a jack sitting near the road who, rather than running at my approach, sat motionless, staring at the setting sun. I continued into town to the one small grocery which welcomed me with cold milk and sandwiches.

The next morning I pedalled into the Pacific Time Zone, and to Baker, only eight miles further. I'd slept in a large quonset hut in Garrison, and dreamt throughout the night that I was back in the Army. As if that wasn't sufficiently unpleasant, a handful of bats began their day as I tried to end mine. Swooping low over my face, I could feel the breeze from their ugly wings.

But now the sun was out, and the Outlaw Bar and Cafe in **Baker** came into view. The owners, Rita and Chuck Berger ("puns are not appreciated"), also operate the Terry Motel and small grocery across the street. Rita is a one-lady Chamber of Commerce, and kept me entertained for half the day with stories of the local scene. Power didn't arrive in Snake Valley until 1970; prior to that 10 kilowatt generators provided the juice. When "salt storms" from the north blew down, they'd turn the land white, and knock out the lights by shorting the circuitry. I heard of flash floods which washed boulders down the highway, and communes (one of polygamists, another of complete communal ownership of property) and a monastery. She knew everyone who came in, and served the tiny community as news station, rumor repository, and historian.

SPUR A—LEHMAN CAVES—(12 miles roundtrip)

Lehman Caves National Monument (changed in 1986 to **Great Basin National Park**) is five miles (all up) west of Baker, and the inexpensive tour makes for a wonderfully cool hour-long escape from the desert heat. The word is that this big cavern (Timpanogos Cave could fit in *one* of its rooms) was discovered by an old cowboy—Absalom Lehman. He was preparing breakfast one day when a pack rat took off with the bacon. Giving chase on his horse, he rode across a piece of ground which, though it looked normal, was merely a thin roof of a huge cave. It supported the pack rat, but gave way under Absalom. Yet all was not lost. Cowboy that he was, his ever-ready lariat was quickly in hand. He lassoed a nearby juniper and hung there, for four days, holding his horse tightly between his legs. Fortunately, a friend happened by before Absalom lost his strength, and they celebrated the discovery of the cave. (I know it *sounds* like a tall tale, but it was told with a straight face.)

Try to spend a day climbing the steep, switch-backed road up Wheeler Mountain. (Baker's elevation is 5318', the road tops out over 10,000', and Wheeler Peak—the highest point in Nevada—is another three thousand feet above that.) There are campgrounds here, a cafe at the cave entrance, and excellent views from the alpine ice field at the top of desolate desert miles toward loop's end a full day's ride away.

Heading back to Delta, ride north out of Baker two miles, until you come to a paved road angling northeast. Follow this five miles to its junction with US 6/50, and make a right. In a few miles you'll come to the Utah border, where an Amoco Station, a small motel, and slot machines are the last

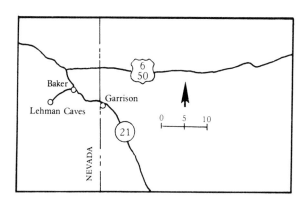

civilization until **Hinckley**, eighty-three miles east. (But Hinckley has no services; it's eighty-nine to Delta from the border.)

I began the ride to Delta with 140 ounces of water, several grapefruits (better than the limes, lemons, oranges, et cetera, that I've tested for desert travel), one pound of cheese, bread, jam, and peanut butter. At **MP 18+** is a nice picnic spot (no water here, or anywhere on this run), one of few along the trail. I ate lunch while crouching in the shade of my saddlebags much later in the day, having just come through a treeless, desolate setting in the Confusion Range. It's desert scrub and alkali, juniper and sage, Notch Peak, Skull Rock Pass, and the Sevier Dry Lake on the way home. I'd seen antelope, a hawk, one eagle, and two coyote pups by **MP 82**. There, the comparatively lush green of Hinckley and **Delta** (six miles east) begins.

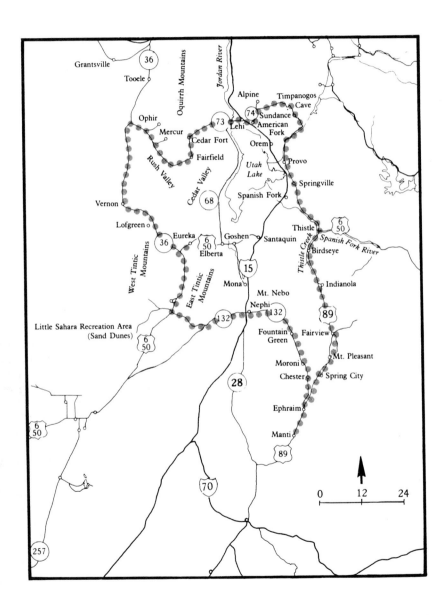

5. UTAH LAKE LOOP

NEPHI—MANTI—PROVO—TIMPANOGOS— FAIRFIELD—VERNON—NEPHI

Mileage: 302

Spur A	FAIRVIEW CANYON	16 miles (roundtrip)	
Spur B	OPHIR	7 "	"
Spur C	SAND DUNES	23 "	"

Mileage: 46

Loop Five is a great one-week, fifty-mile-per-day tour. It boasts desert, green farmland, and a seventeen-mile alpine run around Mt. Timpanogos, home of Timpanogos Cave National Monument. Two LDS temples, a ghost town, a nineteenth-century Stagecoach Inn, the site of Camp Floyd, and the appropriately named Little Sahara Recreation Area (Sand Dunes) also lie along this loop.

Except for the alpine portion, and the hard climb up the Fairview Canyon Spur, this route is not as challenging as some other loops. I've done one long leg of it in winter, the whole of it in early summer, and believe that any season is appropriate for travel. (That is, as long as you are prepared with cold-weather gear, and avoid the alpine portion in winter.) Water is not a problem on this scenic ride, and historical markers and guided tours will explain Pony Express stations, the Dominguez-Escalante Trail, and the military camp which almost overnight created a city of seven thousand people.

Loop Five is centrally located, and runs through many towns and cities.

Thus, one can find many spots to begin and end the tour. During my long summer ride I linked Loops Four and Five together by pedalling east out of Delta on US 50/Utah 125 to Leamington, then riding Utah 132 to the county road coming from Jericho Junction. For this reason, and also because the town is of good size and on a major highway, we begin the loop at Nephi.

The town of **Nephi** (grocery, cafes, motels) has many interesting buildings from different periods in the area's history, but unfortunately has lost much of its charm to the busy highway which feeds into Main Street. There's no real need to provision yourself heavily at this point, for there's a cafe fifteen miles away in Fountain Green, and a grocery and cafe in Moroni, eight miles beyond. Besides, the climb up Salt Creek Canyon is not very difficult.

Ride due east out of Nephi on Utah 132 (it joins Main Street near the north-south midpoint of town), through the narrow canyon alongside Salt Creek, with its oak brush and thick stands of trees. **MP 35** was the first one I spotted, about a mile east of town. But I may have missed one, for my attention was held by a huge flock of sheep which bleated its way slowly through the canyon, taking up both lanes and completely halting traffic. A mile before the summit (**MP 42**) is a plaque which tells of yet another massacre—this one of four pioneers killed by Indians. (I find it difficult to believe, but apparently they were travelling unarmed.)

Shake these unpleasant thoughts by admiring the aspen at the pass and looking toward the row of white-capped mountains ahead. The summit is actually a two-mile level run, and at its end you can see the northern extension of Sanpete Valley. (Numerous power lines, however, do little to enhance this summit ride.) A few exposed red rock ledges serve as faint reminders of other Utah climes, and soon, at **MP 47**, you'll be in **Fountain Green**.

This quiet, pretty place has buildings from many different periods, and a plaque which tells of its abandonment during the Black Hawk War. A hotel opened in 1861, but don't look for a room these days until you come to the larger, more hectic towns further south. I happened to stop for water at the home of Woodrow and Clarisse Talbot before pushing on, and was invited inside for cake and coffee. During an hour of conversation I learned that Mr. Talbot had been on the Civilian Conservation Corps work crew which built the first road to Boulder in the thirties. I told them how I'd nearly been blown off the cliff, was assured I'd meet up with nothing that dramatic on the way to Manti, and pedalled off.

The ride to Moroni is eight miles of level, pleasant travelling. You'll pass some huge turkey farms, where hundreds of the birds sit watching the traffic, and getting fat for fall. I found that by mimicking their calls I could rile the entire bunch into speech, and later, while transcribing my notes from the small tape recorder I carry with me, could barely hear my own words for all their clucking. **Moroni** (**MP 54**, grocery and cafe) has some great old buildings, including an enormous stone barn next to the road. Four miles further south along this level stretch is **Chester** (groceries at a Husky station), then it's nine more to Ephraim. (Traffic is a bit heavier once Utah 132 merges with US 89.) **Ephraim** has all amenities, and some pretty nice folks. I'd rolled out my sleeping bag in a fellow's yard and was grabbing a bite to eat, when an offer came to spend the night in an empty apartment. The manager warned I'd be in the dark, as the electricity was off. It was the first time I'd taken a bath by candlelight.

I toured the town next morning, and discovered the Snow College campus. Riding back to Main Street (US 89) I once again passed buildings which stepped back, in stages, more than a century. Then came the final, level eight-mile ride to **Manti** (motels, cafes, grocery).

What an enchanting place. The LDS Temple sits high on a hill, and dominates the area with its oolite (sometimes called "white sandstone") beauty and wide, green lawns. I admit to fearing that in Utah towns such as this I might run into difficulty, that the people might take exception to my beard and lack of faith and choose to be uncivil. Such a thing happened to me in Jerusalem, when I made the mistake of riding in from the desert on the Sabbath. The looks from those orthodox worshippers with their dark hats and coats, long sidelocks and grave faces were not enjoyable; nor was my response of instant antipathy something I wish to feel again. But not once in Manti did this happen, nor did it occur anywhere else in the state.

The markers in town tell the same story I'd heard in Fountain Green, that the first pioneers had come in late November 1849 and lived in dugouts on what is now Temple Hill. In spring, when things thawed out a bit, the settlers found they were living in a rattlesnake den. Hundreds of the nasty creatures began investigating the unwelcome claimjumpers, who quickly imported hogs to eat the snakes.

It's time to head north. Retrace your steps to the US 89/Utah 132 junction, and veer right. Six miles north of this point is Utah 117; head east on it to the old homes and National Historic District of **Spring City**, then north another four miles to **Mt. Pleasant** (grocery, motel, cafes, and campground nearby). This town has some excellent old buildings and storefronts, a World War I "doughboy" statue, plaques which tell of forts and grasshopper invasions, and the more than a century old Presbyterian Wasatch Academy.

Six miles north is **Fairview** (motel, cafe, grocery), and though I reached this little place via US 89, I was told in town I could have taken a paved backroad (east of 89) all the way from Mt. Pleasant. Fairview, like so many towns nearby, has attractive old storefronts and stone buildings, and though at 6000' it is only five hundred feet higher than Manti, pines grow along the road.

SPUR A—FAIRVIEW CANYON—(16 miles roundtrip)

This is a rather steep (8%) climb in places, and takes you past quaking aspen to Skyline Drive (a north-south, one-hundred-mile, dirt, mountaintop road). I hadn't had a mountain climb in a week or so and therefore welcomed the opportunity, but this ascent is not as pretty as many in the state. Road graders have scarred the earth in places, and several level spots have been widened to allow cars to pull off and admire the view. The result is beer cans and trash; not enough to ruin the ride, but enough to be annoying. Unfortunately, the canyon mouth also has some unsightly trailers and run-down houses which you must pass twice, and thus I suggest you take the much longer and harder, but far more beautiful, Timpanogos Alpine Loop if you only have time for one climb.

A sign at the north edge of Fairview says "Thistle—27 Miles." You'll go up a fair grade for several miles, then level off as you pass a gravel road to Indianola, and a plaque (**MP 264**) which tells of another massacre of whites during the Black Hawk War. It's a pretty run, with mountains and cultivated fields on both sides. Then one descends the canyon to **Thistle**—the meeting place of US 89 and US 6/50. (No services at Indianola, Pines, or Birdseye.)

As of this writing, the town of Thistle and the highway are under water (the result of a massive mudslide, and the backing up of Spanish Fork River). It is claimed that a passable road will soon exist, and that routing cyclists through this canyon should cause no trouble. However, I still wouldn't suggest this path were it not for the fact that bikers always have an alternative unavailable to motorists—overland travel. Several times on my "worlder" I was forced to push my bike around obstacles, and twice I had to carry it through flooded roads. I trust there'll be a paved surface waiting for you at Thistle, but either call ahead to be sure, or plan to do some bushwhacking. (The waters have subsided, and the paved road has been restored. But Thistle, and the cafe where I breakfasted that morning, are gone.)

I slept by the creek just south of Thistle Junction, and the following morning pedalled to a small cafe next to the road. It was a fascinating place for breakfast. I sat there sipping coffee and reading the Dominguez-Escalante journal entry of their trek through this same canyon. Kit Carson, John C. Fremont, Jedediah Smith and many more travelled near here, as also did Spanish traders from Taos (on a northern fork from the main trail) who caused Fremont to apply the name "Spanish Fork" to the region in 1845. My thoughts and the journal before me went back two centuries, while through the cafe door poured modern travellers.

The breakfast, like so many on my rides, took two full hours. I fell into conversation with a motorcyclist who'd been shot down in 'Nam, and still carried shrapnel in his back. I learned he'd been a policeman in a small Kansas town I'd pedalled through on my 1981 winter tour along the Santa Fe Trail. But he'd quit that job like all the rest, and for the same reason. "Nobody but me," said this purebred traveller, "is gonna own *my* time."

I attributed most of this to his close shave overseas, but later found that his wartime experience had merely underscored a lesson learned from his grand-dad. The story was that during the Depression his grandfather had sold the family farm to buy a house in the town. With the house not quite completed, and the sale of the farm already closed, he moved into a hotel for a week and deposited all his money.

"Well," said the grandson, with the demeanor of one who is letting

someone in on a great truth, "he was a rich man on Monday. Then the bank
folded. No farm, no account, and not even enough dough to pay his hotel
bill."

The lesson drawn from this had produced in my acquaintance a thorough-
going disdain for financial security.

"Hell. Who's to say your money's gonna be worth anything tomorrow?
And even if it is—*you* might not be around to enjoy it!"

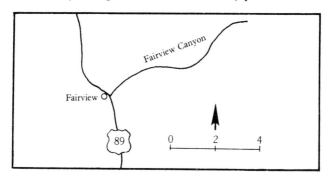

Follow US 89 down canyon for another nine miles, then take the **Spring-
ville** exit and ride north six miles to that town (motels, cafes, grocery) over a
fairly level road.

Continue north another seven miles to **Provo**. This is a big city and has
much to see (refer to Chapter Nine for suggestions), but be careful in the
traffic. Make a right on 900 East Street, at a sign which directs you north to
Brigham Young University. You'll pass by the campus and temple; stay on
900 East as it bends to the west. At the second stoplight you will be on
University Avenue (which further north is called US 189, and takes you up
canyon to the Alpine Loop turnoff). Make a right on University Avenue and
ride the wide shoulder north; there is, after a mile or so, a bike path on the
west side of this street. Stay on this road as it heads out of town and up canyon
for twelve miles to your turnoff.

You'll pass several restaurants on 189, plus **Bridal Veil falls (MP 11+)**,
where there is a tram to the top of the mountain for an unforgettable view.
The canyon also is beautiful, with high, steep walls of rock, rushing water,
and bright green trees and shrubs. But the road is narrow, and carries a heavy
volume of local traffic. Don't stray off the shoulder while admiring the view.

A sign at the turnoff for the Alpine Loop (Mt. Timpanogos, Sundance . . .)
warns of seventeen miles of steep grades and sharp curves. That's true, but
only seven miles of that comes before the summit. There are a couple of level
spots on the way up, the first quite near **Sundance** resort, but it still took me
an hour and forty-five minutes to climb seven miles, without any stops. It's
pines and a sea of aspen near the summit (**MP 18+**), and in fall these quakies
are a shimmering, brilliant yellow.

Watch the hairpin turns as you fly down the other side, and keep an
especially sharp eye out for gravel. Campgrounds are all along this road, and

further down you come to the Visitor Center for **Timpanogos Cave National Monument.** The tour requires a one-and-one-half-mile walk up the mountainside, but is well worth it. For that matter, plan to spend a night on this loop, for trails and sideroads lead to areas of spectacular beauty.

If you're taking Loop Five between November and April (or even during the warmer months if there's been a lot of snow) call the Highway Department for road conditions while you're still in Provo (224-2441). If you find that the Alpine Loop is closed (or if you'd simply like to avoid the climb), pick up US 89 again (500 West Street in Provo) and ride all the way to American Fork. At that point you'll have rejoined the original loop.

If, however, you've taken the mountain road, you'll find there's no food available until you zoom down American Fork Canyon (the canyon the Timpanogos Cave Visitor Center is in), all the way to **Alpine Junction.** This is actually the intersection of Utah 74 and Utah 80. The market at this point is fairly well stocked, but if you're more in the mood for a cafe wait a bit, and enjoy the view of Utah Lake as you run south on 74 four miles to **American Fork** (grocery, cafes).

Main Street in American Fork is Utah 73—your route for the next forty-five miles. Ride west out of town on 73, and follow the signs to **Lehi** (cafes, grocery). Proceed west out of Lehi. You'll pass **MP 37,** then cross the Jordan River, so named because its counterpart in Palestine also runs from a freshwater body (Sea of Galilee) to one of salt (the Dead Sea). After four miles you'll come to Utah 68 (which runs north for twenty-seven miles to Salt Lake City, becoming Redwood Road). If you're pressed for time and have to cut the loop short, turn south on 68 for thirty-five pretty miles along the west shore of Utah Lake, to the tiny town of **Elberta** (a very small market). Head east at this point on US 6/50 three miles to **Goshen,** turn south for ten miles on a small paved road to **Mona,** then proceed south for eight miles more on US 91 to **Nephi.** (Goshen Canyon is *very* pretty.)

But you'll miss a lot of good looking country, and history, if you cut the loop short. From the junction once again of Utah 73/68, at the north end of the lake, ride west. After so much traffic from Thistle Junction to Lehi, it's a relief to return to quiet countryside. After a long pull out of Lehi (a two-summit upgrade) you'll see the sage-covered Oquirrh Mountains, looming above huge fields of wheat in Cedar Valley. Behind you are the snow-capped peaks of the Wasatch Range, and across the lake's blue waters is the supine form of Mt. Timpanogos. Once the long grade is passed you'll have rolling terrain to **Cedar Fort** (11 miles from 68/73)—a little town which has a Husky station on the south end, well stocked with food and cold drinks.

South of Cedar Fort is a scenic six-mile, primarily downhill run to **Fairfield,** which has no services, but does have a lot of history. Pedal through this sleepy little place of poplars and cottonwoods to a sign which directs you eastward off the highway, then on for a block or so to the Stagecoach Inn. Once here, a guided tour and historical markers tell the story.

It's difficult to imagine Fairfield as it once was—the broiling, rip-roaring, third largest town in Utah. This period of its history lasted only three years, from mid-1858 to 1861. General Johnston's troopers, having marched to Utah during the "Mormon War" (see Chapter Three), continued west through Salt Lake to establish Camp Floyd. Immediately, facilities attendant on army bases grew up around the camp, bringing the total population to seven thousand. When General Johnston left to join the Confederacy, the command was transferred to Colonel Cooke—former leader of the Mormon Battalion. (This was a group of some five hundred Mormon men who were persuaded by Brigham Young in 1846 to leave their families at Winter Quarters—a few miles north of present-day Omaha, Nebraska, where preparations were being made for the trek to Utah—and march, via the Santa Fe Trail, to San Diego. The war against Mexico had been declared in May of 1846, and in July of 1847 the Battalion, then in California, was mustered out of service. Colonel Cooke had commanded these men for a large part of the expedition, a trek which is considered by some to be the longest infantry march in American history.) Cooke was ordered east again with his men in 1861, destroyed Camp Floyd, and joined the Union cause against the South. (And, for that matter, against his famous son-in-law, the Confederate general and cavalryman J.E.B. Stuart.)

Be sure to tour the restored Stagecoach Inn (open 12:00 to 6:00 P.M. daily); it also served as a Pony Express station, and as a hotel until 1947. There isn't a great deal to see in the restored Army Commissary Building nearby, but if you return to Utah 73 and make a left you'll come to a road after two hundred yards which turns southeast a quarter-mile, to the Camp Floyd graveyard (a sign on 73 points to it). A wrought-iron fence, green fields, and cedar covered mountains surround this melancholy site.

Back on 73 once more, you'll start off with a gradual five-mile climb to, appropriately, "Fivemile Pass." You now have the beautiful Rush Valley before you. The road curves around the Oquirrh Mountains, past the turnoff for the old mining town of **Mercur** (very little to see). You'll encounter some truck traffic along here, for the mines are operating once again, but there are so few cars on the road that aside from the noise the trucks are not particularly bothersome. Five miles from Mercur (about twelve from Fivemile Pass) is the paved turnoff for Ophir.

SPUR B—OPHIR—(7 miles roundtrip)

The three-and-one-half-mile paved road to **Ophir** is not a tough climb, but what lies at the end makes the effort worthwhile. Many well-preserved nineteenth-century buildings still stand, including the 1870 city hall. Though it was closed when I rode by, I'm told the small market in town has food and cold drinks.

From the Ophir Canyon road it's four miles downhill to the junction with Utah 36. One-half mile north of this intersection is Penney's—a cafe (open all year) with cold beer and great burgers. (Try the Judd's Special.) South on Hwy 36 is a fast, downhill and level run for twenty-one miles to **Vernon** (cafe/market). That is, it's fast if you're not bucking a head wind—unfortunately common in Rush Valley. And a word of caution. From **MP 43** way back at the Utah 73/76 junction, all the way to **MP 28**, there isn't even a farmhouse nearby. Make sure you carry a good supply of water, even in winter.

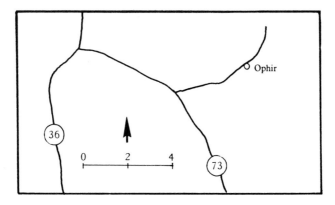

As the road heads east out of Vernon you have a great view of the valley's length to the north, and the mountains on all sides. You'll have to pull a couple of hills the next few miles as you climb out of the valley, and into the rolling area wedged between the East and West Tintic Mountains. Vernon came at **MP 22**; the next place to grab a bite or swig of something wet is at Wild Bill's Bar at **MP 11**, (closed on non-holiday Mondays). Operated by a couple of real nice folks, the place has been around since 1950, and has a large collection of guns on the walls. There's even a pair of leather saddlebags, with the date 1838 stamped on them. And if you're looking for a good place to bed down, a mile further south is an easy-access spot thick with cedars. Just keep your wits about you when you're camping in the wilds—I heard at Wild Bill's that an old tom cougar is often seen around the place.

The mileposts run to zero when you reach the gas station (cold soda) at the intersection of Utah 36 and US 6. Three miles northeast on US 6 is **Eureka**, which has a cafe, a small motel, and a grand fellow named Ray Badertscher at the IGA grocery. (I pedalled in one winter day with six youngsters, met Mr. Badertscher as we reprovisioned, and was invited to dinner at his home. That evening he kept the boys and me entranced with tales of Utah history.)

Heading south again on US 6, you'll have a very scenic, mostly level, and lightly travelled road for fifteen miles, to the turnoff west for the Sand Dunes. Four miles north of that spur road is a rest area—with toilets and drinking water. (First MP after Eureka is 138; rest area is at **MP 128+**.)

SPUR C—SAND DUNES—(23 miles roundtrip)

The long upgrade turnoff for this spur comes just before **MP 121**. It's an eleven-and-a-half-mile ride to the **Oasis Campground**, past the greatest dunes I've seen since my 1974 tour of Egypt. I'd definitely make the trip, if it isn't a busy weekend in spring or summer, for the white sand and green cedar are out of this world—especially at sunset.

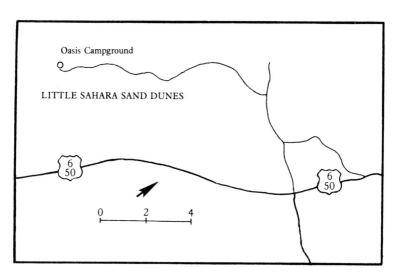

Back to US 6, but this time just to cross it, to take the two-lane blacktop road which angles east-southeast to Utah 132 and Nephi. It's a hilly twenty-seven miles to loop's end from here, but worth every turn of the pedals. The sandy, rocky soil primarily supports sage and juniper, and once you've taken the long grades up, you've earned the fast two-mile descent and lovely view of Juab Valley. This ends the loop, with the fields and white frame houses of **Nephi** in the shadow of twelve-thousand-foot Mt. Nebo to the north.

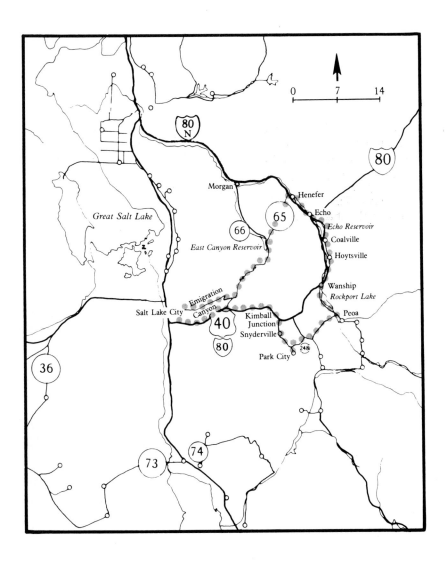

6. EMIGRATION CANYON LOOP

SALT LAKE—HENEFER—COALVILLE—
PARK CITY—SALT LAKE

Mileage: 95

This may be the shortest loop, but it's the longest in Mormon history. It traces the last thirty-five miles of the Mormon Trail into Salt Lake Valley. The Donner Party, Johnston's Army, the handcart pioneers, the Pony Express, the various stagecoach lines, and the transcontinental telegraph also came this way. With such a past, and with its proximity to Salt Lake, this loop should be a favorite.

Be ready for some climbs; for it's not an easy route. You took Little Mountain—at the top of Emigration Canyon—in Loop One. Now you'll ride Big Mountain—the rough, switchback pull which culminates in pines, and precedes the best descent in the state.

You'll pass three reservoirs on this short ride, two of which have campgrounds. Many of the towns along the way have motels, and all have either cafes or a grocery. Drinking water is not a problem, but snow at Big Mountain, from late fall through spring, can cause trouble. I've pedalled over it many times, but the ride I enjoyed the most was when I had to push my bike through snow for two miles at the top. Be prepared in such situations; let someone know where you're going, and take the gear you'll need to make it through the night—just in case.

You'll notice I've not included any spurs. This is because I treat these in my discussion of one- and two-day rides in Chapter Nine. Again, don't let the mileage fool you. Allow three days to see it all, to read the plaques on history and get to know the towns, or to even wet a hook or two.

There's no better way to prepare for this ride than by spending several hours at the first attraction on the loop—Pioneer Trail State Park. It sits across from Hogle Zoo, on Sunnyside Avenue (850 South). The Visitor Center has an excellent tape and mural program which in only a few minutes provides the outline of early Mormon history, and the great trek west. A huge monument commemorates the spot where Brigham Young is said to have looked out over the valley, at the end of the fourteen-hundred-mile trail from Nauvoo, and said, "It is enough. This is the right place...."

Markers explain the figures of fur trappers and early explorers; another tells of the Pony Express riders galloping up this gateway to the East *and* West—Emigration Canyon.

To the north is the "Old Deseret Living History Museum." Still under construction, it already possesses Brigham Young's farmhouse, a cabin built in 1847, a two-story reconstruction of the Salt Lake Social Hall, the Charles C. Rich House, which shows how polygamous families lived beneath a single roof, and much more.

I briefly described Emigration Canyon in Chapter One, and will say only a few words now about its history. Most of it is included in the Pioneer Trail State Park Visitor Center program, and in markers along the way. The first of these plaques tells of "Donner Hill"—the spot where in 1846 the ill-fated Donner Party, after cutting its way through willows down the canyon from Little Mountain, decided they could take no more. Diary accounts indicate as many as fifty or sixty oxen were hitched to *each* of the twenty-three wagons in turn, and dragged over the hill. This seems incredible, especially in light of the fact that the next year, 1847, a Mormon advance team cut its way around the hill in four hours.

Ride slowly up this canyon. Study the overgrowth where the creek runs, and try your best to imagine this foliage stretching completely across the road. It will help you understand Donner's decision to avoid even the last mile or so of cutting their way through, and also serve to make *your* task of pedalling somewhat easier.

Ride past the two cafes and one restaurant and the steep mountainsides of evergreen and oak brush, around what was once called Rattlesnake (now Ruth's) Curve, and on to Little Mountain. Before you is a great descent into Mountain Dell (a "dell" is a small, enclosed, wooded valley), and to the southeast a road which runs to Parleys Canyon. The Donner Party went that way at first, attempting to avoid Little Mountain. But they found Parleys even more impassable, and turned to make the horrible climb.

It's a beautiful view for today's traveller, across the green valley floor of Mountain Dell surrounded by cottonwood and sunflowers, and filled with the calls of meadowlarks. Catch your breath, roll down the hill to Utah 65, and make a left.

From this point you're sixteen miles from Utah 66—the turnoff for East Canyon Reservoir—and only twenty-four from Henefer. But what a climb for the first four or five miles. As you go up, the view back to the west of endless hills and mountain ranges will make you think of what it meant to face them with wagons, and no roads.Your path switchbacks with steeper grades than in Emigration, but fiery-red Indian paintbrush and alpine wild-flowers adorn the roadside, and along with the view, will help to keep your mind off aching legs and lungs.

Finally, the summit. This is Big Mountain, and you're in for one of the great downhill runs in the nation. It goes for miles, so steep in places that you'll have trouble making turns. Once near the bottom it becomes easy pedalling along hillsides filled with sage for three miles to the reservoir.

From the junction of Utah Hwys 65/66 you are eight miles from Henefer, but only two from the campground and marina at **East Canyon** reservoir (both open April through October; marina serves grilled food). At the junction it's left toward the campground, or straight ahead and up a hill to Henefer.

Several historical markers on this part of the ride have lost their metal tablets. They told how the Mormons, after the persecutions in Missouri and Illinois, after the deaths at Winter Quarters, and the great march west, turned south from Weber Canyon to labor up this stretch. And now let's take a moment to think of others who came this way.

This was the route of the Pony Express, during its short lifespan of April 1860 to October 1861. Mail was carried for two thousand miles—between St. Joseph, Missouri, and Sacramento, California—for the regular U.S. postage rate plus five dollars per half-ounce. (This was lowered to one dollar after a few months.) Buffalo Bill Cody, Richard Egan (who later became a Mormon bishop), and many more responded to the advertisement for "young, skinny, wiry fellows, not over 18. Must be expert riders, willing to risk death daily. Orphans preferred ... "A letter made the trip in good time—from eight to fifteen days. And only one rider was lost, killed by Indians. But still the operation lost money, and was put to rest permanently by a less romantic competitor—the transcontinental telegraph.

Some three thousand Mormon handcart pioneers are another group that labored up these hills, from 1856 to 1860. Beginning at Iowa City, Iowa, they pushed and pulled their wooden carts—each one loaded with between one hundred and five hundred pounds—all the way to Utah. The plan was devised when Mormon emigration funds went dry, and worked well for those who made it to Salt Lake before the winter snows. Two groups set out too late, however, and were caught (like Johnston's Army, which also came this way) in heavy winter weather. Some two hundred of them perished.

Ride on to **Henefer** (grocery), and turn right on the main street through town. Follow this across Interstate 84 to the road which runs along the northeast side to the town of Echo. When you first cross over I-84 (also known as I-80N), you'll see a wooden historical marker, which has been made difficult to read by three point-blank shotgun blasts. How sporting.

Weber Canyon's Explorer Trail. Weber Canyon has always been the most important greenway into the valley of the Great Salt Lake. Through its portals passed many important persons of early Utah history, including John Weber, a trapper, who is supposed to have been killed by Indians in the winter of 1828-29, Etienne Provost, who in 1824 reported one of the first explorations of the [Weber] river, and Osborne Russell, who reported explorations in 1841. In 1846 California emigrants took the first wagons down the canyon, encountering . . . hardship and severe losses . . . . In this vicinity the Donner-Reed Party in 1846, which met a tragic fate on the east slope of the Sierras, turned southwest and blazed a trail through the mountains to the Salt Lake Valley. This trail was followed by the Mormon pioneers in 1847, and by the California gold rush emigrants in 1849-50, the Mormon handcart pioneers in 1856, Overland Stage in 1856, and the Pony Express in 1860-61.

The three-mile ride to Echo is very pretty, with deep canyon gorges and high red rock walls to the north, and rolling green mountains to the south. As I pedalled by, engrossed at times in thoughts of early voyagers, a train rolled slowly past. It was the railroad which brought an end to this stream of pioneers; it was a sooty, clanging, but more efficient alternative to horseflesh—and a mode of travel which, in turn, grew obsolete. Cars and trucks raced on the interstate, a plane flew overhead. I rode on, wondering what sort of locomotion man would yet invent.

My slow progress through the canyon was not unlike the pioneers, and thus, like them, I noticed every scent and color, and felt each nuance of geography. I rode past rock formations which reminded me of Goblin Valley, watched a hawk for several minutes circling overhead, and pedalled into **Echo**.

The tiny place has a motel and cafe. Interesting old photos of the area hang around the tables, and the menu offers rabbit (cottontail—not jack). Follow the sideroad out of Echo, around the wind-sculpted portal rocks of Echo Canyon, and ride alongside I-80 (about a half-mile) to the first opportunity to cross under the interstate. A sign points right to Coalville. Make the turn.

But before you do, notice that this road (actually the old highway) continues on the north side of I-80. It runs for ten and a half miles, through a beautiful rock-walled canyon. The road surface is pretty bad, but so few cars use this route that you can move around the holes with ease. It's a very gentle climb (Evanston is thirty-four miles from here, but you can't reach it without jumping on the interstate), and has such scenery! Along the way is another shotgun-peppered wooden sign on local history. (See Chapter Three for more information on the "Mormon War.")

In 1857, due to false official reports and other misrepresentations, US troops under Albert Sidney Johnston, were sent to suppress a mythical "rebellion" among the Mormons. Brigham Young, then governor, exercising his constitutional rights, forbade the army to enter Utah on the grounds that there was no rebellion, and that he had not been officially informed of the government's action in sending the troops. Strategic places between Fort Bridger and Salt

Lake City were fortified. Remnants of these fortifications can be seen on the tops of the cliffs through this section of Echo Canyon. [sign damage] . . . Fort Bridger and Fort Supply, then in Utah and owned by the Church, were burned. Following negotiations between Governor Young and Captain Van Vliet, and mediation of Colonel Thomas L. Kane, the army was held east of Fort Bridger during the winter of 1857-58, and entered Utah without opposition the next spring. It was recalled at the outbreak of the Civil War.

And now back to the underpass, at the canyon mouth. The road runs beneath the highway, then twists around and climbs a hill. From here you'll see the pretty blue of Echo Reservoir. It's a nice ride along the lake to Coalville; not much traffic, and the noise of the interstate is too far away to be heard. A tiny store is found at Echo Resort on the water's edge, but **Coalville** lies only five miles from the I-80 underpass, and has all amenities.

Spend some time looking around. Old homes, attractive architecture, and a courthouse built in 1903, make the visit pleasant. The town also has a health center with an emergency room. And there's a seventeen-mile one-way run to Pineview, a climb which is rough in places—no services there, or in Upton. Though scenic, I wouldn't choose to pull the hill except as practice. There are far better tours nearby.

Farm sights and smells abound along the pleasant three-mile ride to **Hoytsville,** and further south to where this two-lane road crosses the interstate once again. Actually, there are two roads angling over I-80. The first one is where the main road splits; it rolls down a slight hill toward the highway, while a smaller blacktop road lies ahead and to the left a bit. Take either one; the second continues south to where a yellow sign says "Dead End," then zips off to the right, beneath the interstate, and comes out at the Spring Chicken Inn.

This intriguing restaurant lies on the edge of **Wanship**, which has a market as well. Continue through town on the main road as it curves to run beneath the highway once more. You're now on US 189, and will pass another market just after the interstate. (Don't get any ideas about the paved road which heads uphill toward Salt Lake on the *north* side of I-80. It goes a short way and ends.) You'll have a good pull past the Rockport spillway, but once at the top the view of white sails and seagulls on the water is refreshing. The Rockport Reservoir campground is open April through October, and the marina has a restaurant.

Once you've taken the first hill to the reservoir, the remainder of the six-mile run from Wanship to your turnoff a mile north of Peoa is a snap. However, the road leading west for seven miles to US 40 is not so easy. A couple of sharp climbs and a quick descent, and you're on US 40. Make a right (head north) for a mile and a half to the junction with Utah 248. Ride this to **Park City**, and treat yourself to some time in town.

For the final run to Salt Lake, refer to Chapter One, and follow Utah Hwys 248/224 to Kimball Junction, then ride side roads that parallel the interstate, finishing upon the shoulder of I-80 from Parleys Summit west.

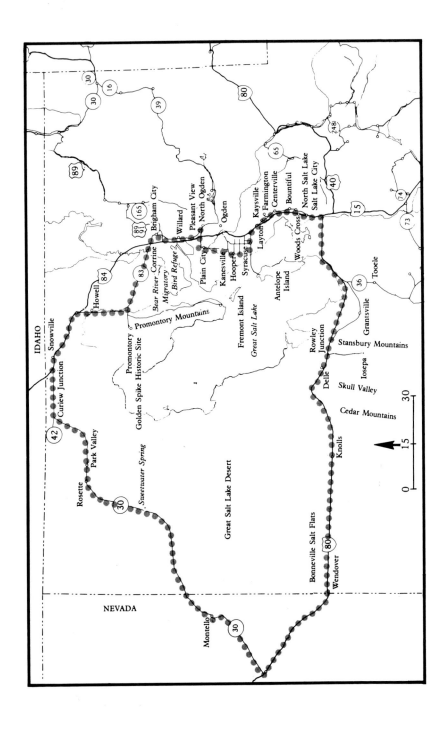

7. GREAT SALT LAKE LOOP

SALT LAKE—OGDEN—SNOWVILLE—
MONTELLO (NEV.)—WENDOVER—
SALT LAKE

Mileage: 420

Spur A	ANTELOPE ISLAND	20 miles (roundtrip)	
Spur B	PROMONTORY		
	PENINSULA	44 "	"
Spur C	GOLDEN SPIKE	16 "	"

Mileage: *80*

    I have a difficult time writing about this loop. For while it is extremely historical, and very scenic along its eastern edge, its northern and southern legs are long, bare, dry, and lonely. You have to want to experience what the early travellers overcame, or simply wish to rack up miles.

    It's tricky getting to North Ogden from Salt Lake without riding hectic US 89, but it can be done. After that, directions are pretty simple; for most of the route you're on the only road around. There is little traffic in most places, settlements are far apart, the landscape barren with few rough climbs. But while few cars pass in a day's riding on the north leg, there's no alternative to a hundred miles of interstate on the southern stretch. There are cafes, fruit stands, and restaurants galore at Brigham City, but after that there are many miles between water holes.

There are benefits, however. The unchanging landscape aids the imagination, and makes it easier to empathize with the ones whose paths you're following. Look out over the Salt Lake and summon up Jim Bridger for a moment, who in 1826 sailed the waters in a bullboat. Progressing from stretched buffalo hide hulls to India rubber, Kit Carson and John Fremont paddled about in 1843. Before them, for centuries, Indians were along the shore, and after Bridger's discovery of the lake in 1824 came Peter Skene Ogden, Jedediah Smith and Joseph Walker (on separate trips to California), the 1841 Bartleson-Bidwell wagon train, the Donners, the Mormon Battalion returning from the west coast, and the anxious forty-niners heading there. You'll ride through a town where a cabin built in 1846 still stands, past the site where the transcontinental railroad was completed, and by an unlikely valley of sand and salt which a colony of Hawaiians once called home.

It's a long five hundred miles of riding, too hot for comfort in summer, but not impossible to travel then, or anytime. I learned in June what it's like to be nearly out of water on the Salt Flats in the sun. And though I felt one with the Donners, I suggest that you forego that historical homage, and travel in spring or fall.

I mentioned that riding side roads from Salt Lake to North Ogden is difficult, but possible. So bear with me as we negotiate a confusing stretch of unnamed roads and underpasses.

My choice for travelling north out of Salt Lake is to climb poorly surfaced State Street to Capitol Hill, then turn west on Third North, directly in front of the Capitol, and ride one block to Columbus Street, which in three blocks becomes Victory Road. Proceed on Victory Road down the long hill to its link-up with Beck Street (US 89), and continue north. (Spend a little time on Capitol Hill—the Statehouse and Pioneer Museum both warrant visits.) If you wish to avoid Capitol Hill, however, ride north on 200 West Street. It will curve to meet with 300 West, which is the in-town extension of Beck Street (and US 89). Ride past the old Municipal Baths building (now the Salt Lake Children's Museum) and the Warm Springs historical monument, and continue north.

Beck Street is very busy during rush hour, and forces you to cross several sets of railroad tracks. To escape the traffic I usually ride a small parallel road (on the east side) which begins just before **MP 20**—though during the day you have to contend with rock-carrying trucks, and areas of hard-packed dirt. (The trucks come from the quarries and a cement plant which you pass on the way to Bountiful.) There are oil refineries and scrapyards to the west, and thus the first ten miles are not very scenic.

About three hundred feet after this side road ends, at the top of a slight hill, which corresponds with the North Salt Lake exit of I-15, a road called

Orchard Drive angles off to the northeast. Ride this road through **North Salt Lake** and **Bountiful**; though busy at times and in places poorly surfaced, it is primarily residential. Orchard Drive takes you east, then north again, providing a great view of the mountains and the lake. The road becomes 400 East as you continue into **Centerville**. (Bountiful has a motel, grocery stores, and many restaurants; Centerville has several drive-ins and a restaurant. These communities also have attractive old stone homes and buildings.)

On the north edge of Centerville you come to a point where a right or left turn are the only options; turn left (west—toward the lake, away from the mountains) and ride downhill for two blocks to the town's main street. Make a right and continue north. Stay on this road as it runs through **Farmington** (grocery, and great nineteenth-century homes) where it is called 200 East, then 100 East, then State Street, and finally Utah 106, as it curves about. Follow 106 as it turns west toward US 89 and ends. Continue west on the same road (now unnamed) as it heads under the highway, and after a mile or so takes you up a hill to the Frontage Road of I-15. Ride north on this smoothly paved road; it becomes 50 West Street when it reaches **Kaysville** (motel, campground, cafe, grocery). Proceed north past Barnes Bank, the Kaysville Library and City Hall, to a sign which points left to Utah 273.

Proceed to Utah 273 left (west) and ride under I-15, past two sets of railroad tracks, to a "T" in the road. Turn right (north) and continue until the first paved road comes in on the left. Make a left and follow this road as it turns north (great views of mountains and lake again, and many farms), crosses Gentile Street and Gordon Road, and runs north to Utah 108 (also called 1700 South). Make a left onto 108 and roll west (past a small market) for about seven miles, to the junction of Utah Hwys 110/127 (110 runs north from here; 127 is the number given the seven-mile causeway running out to Antelope Island. It is actually an extension of 108).

SPUR A—ANTELOPE ISLAND—(20 miles roundtrip)

This spur is a must. The smell of salt water, the gulls and avocets and long-billed curlews swooping from blue skies to even bluer water, the frothy white foam lapping against the causeway as you pedal out—where else can you get this and much more for such little effort? At the island there is a slight admission fee which entitles you to all facilities—swimming, showers, camping, but no food. Besides, the view of the Wasatch from the island is wonderful, especially in winter.

Fremont and Kit Carson camped on the site of Salt Lake City in October of 1845, then visited this island, which is the lake's largest. While there they killed a few antelope and saw many more. These first known visitors thus blessed the place with what seemed an appropriate name. (When they returned to shore they met an Indian who said he owned the island; Fremont paid the man for the antelope slain and eaten.)

A handout at the State Park gate says that the lake's salt content fluctuates between fourteen and twenty-seven percent (due to water level differences), compared with three percent for the ocean. Fremont, during an earlier visit in 1843, determined the percentage through the age-old method of making salt. He wrote in his journal:

> Roughly evaporated over the fire, the five gallons of water yielded fourteen pints of very fine-grained and very white salt, of which the whole lake may be regarded as a saturated solution.

*Once again the vicissitudes of nature alter our path, for the lake has risen so much as to submerge this road completely.

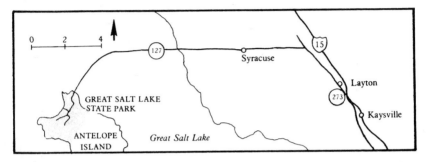

Returning from Antelope Island, turn left (north) on Utah 110 (4500 West Street)—the first major paved road encountered on your left after the causeway. After approximately three and a half miles you'll come to a "T" in the road; make a left (west) and continue as it curves north again and leads to **Hooper** (dairy, snack bar) at the junction of east-west Utah 98.

Utah 110 has changed into Utah 37. This road runs north, east, then north and east again on its way to **Kanesville** (market), then meets a highway (two-lane blacktop road, as are all of these) numbered Utah 40 on most maps, but whose signs name it Utah 134. Another sign at this junction points north to **Plain City** (cafe, grocery) about eight miles away. Ride north on 134 past the Country Corner store at the junction of Utah 39, then on to Plain City.

This has all been level riding, over roads of little traffic, past farmhouses, new subdivisions, and little towns of very old buildings. Remain on 134 as it heads east out of town, jags north a bit, and then rolls due east for several miles to run beneath I-15 and on to US 89. Turn right (south) on 89 for one-eighth of a mile, then left (east) on Utah 235. Proceed east on 235 for several blocks to the main street (Washington Blvd.) of **North Ogden** (market, cafe). Here it is south to the city of **Ogden** (all amenities, plus the "living history" museum of Fort Buenaventura—built in the 1840s), or north (left) to a "T" in the road at the north end of town. A right turn here goes east to Liberty and Pineview Reservoir; a left turn takes you out of town on Elberta Drive, which after a couple miles is called Pleasant View Drive. This road then angles north-northwest to join US 89. At the Pleasant View/89 junction is a historical marker on one of the very early fur trappers.

Peter Skene Ogden, son of a Loyalist of the Revolutionary War days who fled to Canada as a British sympathizer, was one of the most courageous and gallant of the fur trappers, traders, and explorers of the early West. In the struggle between the United States and Great Britain for supremacy in the Rocky Mountains. [This sentence fragment has not been miscopied. Several times throughout the state I found markers with such problems, including— as below—misspellings.] Ogden was chief field captain for the powerful British-owned Hudson's Bay Fur Company. He was charged with over-trapping the Rocky Mountains to discourage the westward-advancing Americans. In May of 1825 a party of American trappers confronted Ogden at nearby Mountain Green, informed him falsely that he was on American soil, and ordered him to leave. Ogden stanchly defended his rights in this yet unceded territory but was forced to withdraw when twenty-three of his men deserted with approximately eight hundred beaver pelts. Unusual among trappers Ogden was literate, and left an excellent journal of his struggles in Utah where Ogden City, Ogden Canyon, and Ogden Valley now honor his name.

US 89 at this point is four lanes wide, with nice shoulders. It's only five miles to **Willard** (cafe, grocery), and seven miles beyond that to **Brigham City** (all amenities). Traffic is usually not heavy, for I-15 carries most of it, and the nearby mountains and many fruit stands make this an enjoyable stretch of riding. (Two miles south of Brigham City is Maddox Steak House, a large and reportedly excellent restaurant.)

One mile south of Brigham is the US 89/Utah 13 junction; US 89 goes east to Logan, 13 continues northeast to Brigham City. Once in town you'll see the huge sign for the Bear River Migratory Bird Refuge, about sixteen miles due west. This area of salt marshes is a wonderful place for bird sightings, but the roads which circumnavigate the Refuge headquarters are dirt and gravel—terrible for touring (but great for mountain) bikes. Remain on the same street through town, passing the beautiful 1876 Box Elder Tabernacle, and a statue dedicated to the dead of World Wars I and II. (This statue comes at Forest Street. A small sign nearby points west to the Bird Refuge.) Across the street from this crouched infantryman is the Idle Isle— an excellent old restaurant which has been in business since 1921, and is similar in style to Lamb's Grill in Salt Lake, and the Bluebird in Logan. (The lake's rise has closed this beautiful refuge for the present.)

If you aren't in the mood for a meal, but would like something before you head out of town, stop at the dairy three blocks north of the Idle Isle, on the main street you've ridden all the way through Brigham—Utah 13. The dairy is on the east side of the street, makes its own ice cream and a mean chocolate malt, and has an old-style fountain.

The road surface in Brigham, and for a few miles beyond, is poor. You'll see a sign on the north edge of town pointing west to the Golden Spike National Historic Site, thirty relatively level miles away. Follow this road, 13/83, as it runs under I-15 and on to **Corrine** (no motel or grocery). You'll pass the Oriental and American Cafe, a name which points to the number of Chinese, and later Japanese, who worked on railroad gangs in Utah and elsewhere in the West. Corrine, the first non-Mormon town in Utah, was founded in 1869. It led a fast and promising life at first, with dance halls, brothels, saloons, a large hotel, and opera house, and for a time was thought perfectly situated to eclipse even Salt Lake City. But other railroad lines were soon constructed which ended most of the rail traffic through town. A diphtheria epidemic added to the economic woes, and helped bring on the end of another western boomtown.

It's a pretty ride west of Corrine on 83 (Hwy 13 has turned north), through Bear River Valley where once, in the fall of 1824, Jim Bridger plodded his way to the shores of the great lake to dip his hand into the waters, taste a finger, and conclude he'd found "an arm of the Pacific Ocean." The marsh smells and birdsong are lovely here, and will seem sweeter still when you reach the desolation coming up. Unfortunately, I'd timed my ride along this stretch in late afternoon, and soon faced a hundred cars racing past me in the other lane. It was shift change at Thiokol, the huge facility fifteen miles west of Corrine, described by my waitress in Brigham as "the biggest-ever rocket plant." More accurately, it is the largest plant involved in the "research, development and manufacture of solid-propellant rocket motors." I'd also been informed that the space shuttle boosters, after being retrieved from the ocean, are hauled here for refueling. Amazing. I would pass a plant dedicated to the space age while on my way to Golden Spike National Historic Site. There, on May 10, 1869, the final track was laid connecting the East and West by rail. One hundred years later, a man stood on the moon.

As you pedal around the southern tip of the Blue Springs Hill you'll come to a turnoff (just as 83 angles north) to the Historic Site, and to Promontory Peninsula which juts southward into the lake. Take the turnoff west, and ride for two miles over level ground to a junction. The spur leading out to Golden Spike jags right, then continues west (follow the signs) up one of the roughest climbs of this loop; the paved road which runs due west a half-mile and then south for twenty-two is the peninsula run.

SPUR B—PROMONTORY PENINSULA—(44 miles roundtrip)

This spur is a beauty. Nicely surfaced, almost no traffic, occasional marshland to the east, crag-topped mountains on the west, plus fantastic views of the lake and the Wasatch mountains are yours for a few hours pedalling. There are a couple of rough hills, but overall not much climbing on this approach to Fremont Island. Fremont, Kit Carson, and four others paddled out to it in a rubber boat in September of 1843. Finding it "perfectly barren," they named it "Disappointment Island," scratched a cross on a slab of rock (still visible today), and sailed off. Carson relates the short return trip to shore in his *Autobiography*:

> We had not gone more than a league when the clouds commenced gathering for a storm. Our boat was leaking wind, and one man was continually employed at the bellows. Fremont urged us to pull for our lives, saying that if we did not reach the shore before the storm commenced we would surely all perish. We did our best, and arrived in advance of the storm. We had scarcely landed when it commenced, and within an hour the waters had risen eight or ten feet.

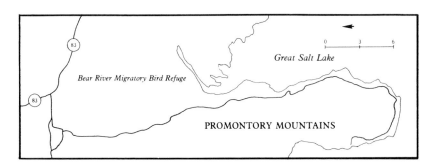

Green grass and bluish sage provide a colorful blanket for the hillsides, while ducks and other waterfowl find this peaceful place a perfect nesting site. After twenty-two miles you'll reach a sign which warns you're at the end of public lands.

SPUR C—GOLDEN SPIKE—(16 miles roundtrip)

Returning north from the peninsula, make a left back at the junction and proceed west for seven miles to the Golden Spike Historical Site. The Visitor Center and various plaques tell the story of uniting the nation by rail. Some twelve thousand Chinese laid track for the Central Pacific, while many of the Union Pacific men were Irish.

Many of the Chinese settled throughout the West once the railroad had been completed, finding work in mines, restaurants, laundries, and other businesses, and creating "chinatowns" where they congregated. Salt Lake hosted one such neighborhood in the Plum Alley area near Main Street and First South. The 1900 census reported almost three hundred Chinese living there.

Follow Utah 83 north through Blue Creek Valley, past high grass near the water, and mountains to the west. I spooked a deer, a skunk, and a huge flock of noisy blackbirds as I pedalled by, and after a while spotted a church steeple in the tiny town of **Howell**. Looking at the map, you'll see a reportedly paved road leading due north through the valley, and past Blue Creek Reservoir to Interstate 84. (It veers off from 83 when the latter jags east.) I had to take 83 to the interstate in order to see what was available in Howell (no services), but was told the straighter valley road would have saved me several miles.

The pretty, quiet ride from Thiokol was over as I boarded the wide shoulder of the interstate. Concerned about approaching darkness, I pedalled quickly, and was on a fast downgrade when a car pulled alongside. A bright red Pontiac kept pace as it edged near the shoulder, and two twenty-year-old long-haired heads looked my way.

"Where the hell you goin'?!"

I told them.

"Where you been?"

I gave them a three-sentence rundown of my trails, while wondering when the driver was going to swerve into me. They seemed to find it incredible that a cyclist could cover more than two thousand miles in a single month.

"Good God!" said the driver, still not looking at the road. "No *wonder* you're so skinny! Pull over."

Trying to take this as a compliment, I considered the command. They probably want to talk, I thought, while in the recesses of my mind rose the nagging doubts of modern society—drug-crazed kids who'll hock my bike for a fix, amoral youth raised on a steady diet of televised crime. There was no reason for concern if they didn't have weapons, for my trusty blade was in my pocket, and a grenade-like grapefruit lay in my handlebar bag. But what if they had a Saturday night special?

I pulled over, stopped, and smiled. First line of defense. Kill 'em with kindness. Besides, no matter what happened at least I wouldn't be run over. The fellow riding shotgun had a crazy grin, and as he reached beneath the front seat with one hand, kept his eyes on me and spoke.

"What *you* need is a silver bullet!"

Great. I was going to be killed by an addict who thought he was the Lone Ranger. My mind raced—do I go for the grapefruit and try to bean him, or hope that his aim from twelve inches away is poor enough to only maim me? Indecision held me motionless. I'd go out frozen in place, smiling at my murderer like an idiot. His hand came up from beneath the seat, then jerked toward me.

"Here!" he said, "Have one on us!"

It was a shiny silver aluminum can of light beer.

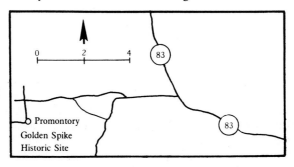

The last twenty miles of interstate before **Snowville** is a series of long grades up and down, as wide valleys stretch far away to the west. The town comes a half-mile past **MP 8**, and has a small motel and several cafes (one of which also sells groceries). I asked a lady if I could roll out my sleeping bag on her lawn, petted the family mutt, was well-licked in return, and walked to Mollie's Cafe.

An interesting hour's conversation followed, as I fell in with a haying team chowing down before work. They all looked hashed, and explained they were trying to get enough coffee inside to provide a good long buzz. The shifts were forty-eight hours on, twenty-four off, with only the huge bright lights of the combines to keep the dark at bay. "After twenty-four you can't steer straight," one fellow said. "You oughta see them fields in mornin'. Look like a giant snake ate its way through the hay."

They were a rough, kind bunch, who in their camaraderie and humor reminded me of good platoons I'd known overseas. I watched them down their NoDoz tablets with final slugs of java, and made note of their suggestions for my long trek west: don't ride the roads at night, for the rattlers stretch out across the pavement for warmth; there'll be "sweetwater" halfway between Rosette and Montello—but watch for rattlers there as well.

Leave Snowville on Utah 30/42, which parallels the interstate at first. You've got only a few hard pulls to face all the way back to Salt Lake, and will have an end-on view of the white-capped Raft River Mountain range as you pedal to Curlew Junction. Utah 30 drops south (42 goes to Idaho) to loop around the ten-thousand-foot peaks, through desert scrub north of an area of salt flats. The first milepost past Snowville is **90**; **Curlew Junction** is reached at **MP 75**. In early summer Indian Creek (**MP 63**) flows quickly down the mountainsides and under the road, granting life to junipers, cliffrose and mountain mahogany.

The little town of **Park Valley** comes at **MP 56+**, and on its west side is the "Overland Trail Motel," campground, and grocery, with hot Lakeshire sandwiches. The nice old grandmother at the cash register took time to warn me not to make the ride out west, but if I "wasn't going to listen at least look out for snakes." She meant the same area of sweetwater springs, fifteen miles past Rosette (no services).

Utah 30 runs due west toward the pretty Grouse Creek Mountains, then turns for twenty-five miles to scoot around their southern flank. The very welcome spring comes at **MP 30**, and after all the warnings I was almost sad not to do battle with a rattler. A historical marker tells of earlier travellers, who also slaked their thirst at this watering hole. Jedediah Smith—killed in 1831 by Comanches on the Santa Fe Trail—came this way in 1826, the year he travelled around the Great Salt Lake's eastern edge, then headed south and west to California. Peter Skene Ogden also came by here early in the century. Joe Walker, a "tough as a hickory knot" mountain man, chosen in 1833 to lead a party to California, also drank here. (Who chose him? It was Benjamin Louis Eulalie de Bonneville, whose mother fled Napoleonic France with him when he was still a boy, who graduated from West Point in 1815, and was later a Seventh Infantry U.S. officer and explorer in the West. It is *his* name which is applied to the ancient lake and salt flats.)

The first wagons to cross Utah were part of the Bartleson-Bidwell Party which passed this spring in 1841, on the way to California. The group actually expected to strike rivers running west from the Salt Lake (not knowing this was the undrained Great Basin), and to build boats if necessary to float to San Francisco. Instead, with thick tongues and few belongings they trudged across the deserts, to finally reach the San Joaquin Valley on pack animals. The wagons remained behind in Utah mud and Nevada sand.

Finally, some of the gold-seeking forty-niners came this way, on their trek to Sutter's Mill. Those who could afford it took clipper ships around the Horn to California. Those with less booked passage to Panama (then still part of Colombia), walked across the Isthmus jungles to the other side, and boarded another ship for the final leg of travel. And those with least of all merely turned their horses west, applied the spurs, and made it if their luck held out.

So much history, but such bleak scenery. The heat on my summer ride around Loop Seven was so intense that by the time I reached **Montello** (11 miles into Nevada—45 from the spring, and 109 from Snowville), I had only one swig of water left. Montello is a tiny place, but does have a motel and cafe, and a grocery store which is closed on Sundays. (I happened to be there on the Sabbath, but the owner opened it for me.)

10,716' Pilot Peak is less than twenty miles southeast of town. Your road doesn't run to it, but some of those who travelled earlier took sight on the mountain and made it to the springs which feed the vegetation near the mountain's base. After those life-saving waters came more desert miles, and at last the high Sierras.

A long, gradual pull and a short steep climb await you after Montello, and then, nearly forty miles from town, Interstate 80 can be seen. At the junction of Nevada 30 and I-80 is a Chevron Station, good for water and pretzels, but little else. It sits next to the now-defunct Oasis Cafe, and the cyclist must pedal the remaining thirty-two miles to Wendover before he can sit down to a meal. The terrain isn't difficult, but I wish you better luck with winds than I had throughout the loop. It seemed no matter which direction I was headed the wind was always in my face.

Wendover has motels, cafes and restaurants, a grocery store, and casinos. About two miles north of town is the Danger Cave State Historical Monument. There's little to see here, but excavations indicate that human habitation of the site goes back ten thousand years. Also nearby are the Bonneville Salt Flats where land speed records are set on the ancient bed of Lake Bonneville. Rest up in town, pack your bike with all the water and grapefruits it will hold, and get ready for the 123 miles back to Salt Lake City.

You'll notice a frontage road along the interstate at first, attractive for its distance from the noise of cars and trucks. I called the Highway Patrol and asked how far it went. "All the way to Knolls—40 miles," I was told. Well, maybe it does. But I'd have had to sift through sand to find it.

I headed out in early morning, hoping to be in Salt Lake in twelve hours, and looked forward to the first quiet stretch on the frontage road. After a few miles a sign gave the encouraging message "No Maintenance Done—Travel at Your Own Risk." They weren't kidding. Another mile and the road was so filled with sand and gravel that I decided to cross to the interstate. That is when I learned first-hand what emigrant diarists meant by "desert mud."

The gray-white surface misleads one into thinking it will support anything, but only some portions (like the Salt Flats mentioned above) ever dry out sufficiently. Instead, a sticky goo of mud clutches at everything—my feet and ankles as I carried my bike across, the one car I saw which had gone off the highway and gotten mired, and the wagon wheels of those who followed the suggestions of a man called Hastings.

Lansford Warren Hastings was probably the most cursed man in emigrant history. There was good cause. In 1846, for reasons of personal gain, he convinced several California-bound wagon trains that his "cutoff" from Fort Bridger (along the southern end of the Great Salt Lake) was a faster, better route. The normal path was the Oregon Trail to southern Idaho, then south into Nevada, the Humboldt and Truckee Rivers to the Sierras, then up and over that last monstrous barrier. Some sixty wagons in the Harlan-Young and Lienhard parties did make it across the Salt Flat, but the Donner-Reed Party left later in the season. They lost fifteen days just getting from Henefer to Salt Lake (see Loop Six), and expected only half the roughly eighty miles without water across the desert you're now riding. Sun-crazed livestock wandered off to die, five wagons were abandoned to the mud. But most important was the lost time, and the weariness of those animals which did make it across.

More problems arose. While on the Humboldt, stock was lost to the Paiute Indians. An ox-beating brought on a fight between two men, which ended with young John Snyder dead—a knife plunged in his chest. Then came early winter snows. In late October they could go no further, and made camp in the Sierra near the lake which bears their name. The wagon train was eighty-seven people strong when it made its way through the Rockies; only forty-seven were to come through the Sierras with their lives. Diaries tell of freezing cold, frostbite, and starvation. And they tell as well of the lengths to which people will go to stay alive. First lifestock, then pets, then:

Mrs. Murphy said here yesterday . . . she would Commence on Milt. and eat him. The Donnos [Donners] . . . told . . . folks that they commence to eat the dead people 4 days ago . . . .

Twelve-year-old Virginia Reed survived, and summarized the lesson learned in a single sentence. Writing to her cousin back east she warned "never take no cutofs and hury along as fast as you can."

Ten miles or so east of Wendover is a rest stop with water. Indian women often sit here with their wares of jewelry spread out on blankets before them. A plaque tells of the first transcontinental telephone line being connected nearby in 1914. And then a sign a short distance from the rest stop—"Knolls 32 Salt Lake City 111."

Knolls comes at **MP 40**, and has a small cafe. More importantly, it's the last source of water for thirty-seven miles. At **MP 54+** is a marker telling of Hastings Pass (through the Cedar Mountain range), along the Donner route. A cafe is present at **Rowley Junction (MP 76+)**. The highway here leads south to Iosepa—an 1889 settlement founded by Hawaiians who had been converted to the Mormon faith. A small leper colony was established when the disease appeared among a few of the more than two hundred settlers. By 1916 almost all had returned to their islands.

From Rowley Junction east to Salt Lake City is another forty miles of salt flats, mountain ranges to the south, and good views of the lake. Water sits on both sides of the road in places, supporting several species of birds which are a pleasure to watch—especially after such lifeless miles. The map will indicate alternatives to I-80 into town, depending on just where you wish to go. On the final stretch is another cafe—this one a huge truckstop at the Tooele exit (**MP 99**). I'd fought a head wind all day long, and went inside to rest.

Sitting in the air-conditioned comfort, I toasted the memory of the loop with my root beer float, then saddled up for the final miles to home.

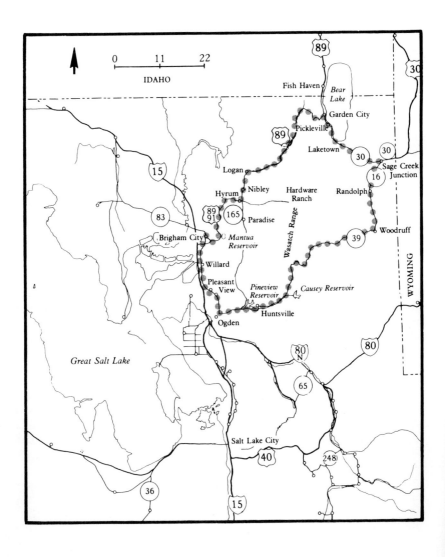

8. BEAR LAKE LOOP

OGDEN—WOODRUFF—
SAGE CREEK JUNCTION—BEAR LAKE—
LOGAN—HYRUM—BRIGHAM CITY—OGDEN

Mileage: 188

Spur A HARDWARE RANCH   32 miles (roundtrip)

Loop Eight is a short, late spring through fall ride over several mountain passes—one of which is nine thousand feet high. The alpine scenery and cool temperatures, plus the water of many reservoirs and Bear Lake make this a very pleasant summer tour. But a warm sleeping bag will be needed if you plan to see the birch and aspen turn brilliant yellow, for nights in early fall usually bring on morning frost.

All of northern Utah's major cities lie along this loop, and distances between food and water are relatively short. Motels, many campgrounds, and miles of pine and fir forest make bedding down an easy chore. As to direction of travel, I suggest you allow your departure time to determine that. Try to avoid riding up Sardine, Logan, or Ogden Canyons late on Friday afternoons, or down them when traffic is returning home. I've tried to gauge which climbs are easier, but there's no significant difference. While the steep pull from Bear Lake to Geneva Summit (on the way to Logan) is the hardest climb, and would tend to suggest a clockwise ride due to easier Logan Canyon, the reasoning fails. This is because the Laketown–Sage Creek Junction run is harder in this direction.

This portion of the Wasatch, plus Cache Valley and Bear Lake, were well known to fur trappers as early as the 1820s. The annual mountain man rendezvous was held at Bear Lake in 1827, and was where the Blackfeet and whites removed many scalps in battle. Condominiums now sit where arrows once flew and black powder musket smoke curled up from gun barrels. Enjoy the luxuries available where the developers have been, for there is still enough untouched to enflame the imagination. Look out over Bear Lake, peer into the trees, and summon forth Beckwourth, Bridger, and Jedediah Smith.

The "living history" Fort Buenaventura State Park in **Ogden**, and the Browning Arms Museum there will give you an idea of what once was necessary to traverse this area. Stock up with food (it's more expensive at the trading posts near Pineview Reservoir), and head up Ogden Canyon. (Twelfth Street becomes the Canyon Road.) There's little room for two lanes and the river which gushes past, so be careful as you look at the steep rock walls and cottonwoods along the banks. It's seven pretty miles to the reservoir, which has campgrounds, beaches, food, and other facilities expected at a recreation area (except for a motel).

Take a couple of hours to visit the **Huntsville** Trappist Monastery, where thirty-five monks live and worship in a beautiful agricultural setting several miles from the main road. You'll pass an American Legion Hall on Utah 39 as you round the reservoir's southeast arm; make a right on the first road after the Hall and ride east for two miles. When you reach a "T" in the road a sign saying "Monastery" directs you south another mile to the chapel and meeting room. You'll be allowed to talk with only one or two monks, for the remainder live a secluded life of work and prayer. (The Trappist branch of the Cistercian order, established in France in 1664, is known for its austerity.) Delicious bread and honey can be purchased in the meeting room, and the public is allowed to observe prayer services from a chapel balcony.

Return to 39, by riding north on the last road which brought you to the Monastery, then make a right and climb for twenty miles or so to the summit at more than nine thousand feet. You'll pass campgrounds and the Causey Reservoir turnoff early in the climb, and finally come to the Monte Cristo campground (open June through September; drinking water available during those months) near the summit. Then comes a twenty-five-mile descent— so gradual toward the end that pedalling is required. (Woodruff, at 6340', is more than two thousand feet higher than Ogden.) You'll find the east side of the range far more sparse than the west, but red soil, trees, and sage provide a pretty view.

Woodruff has a small market (north of the intersection of Utah Hwys 39/16). Ride north for ten level miles, past irrigated fields and sage-covered expanses, to the larger town of **Randolph**. Two cafes, a small motel and market, and some friendly people await you there. Then it's rolling terrain for nine miles north to **Sage Creek Junction** (no services), where a sharp eye will often spot antelope.

The map indicates only twelve miles from Sage Creek to Laketown, but don't plan to make it in an hour's easy pedalling. You'll climb through tan-colored grasses for about a thousand feet—first a slight grade, then a bit rougher pull, and then a sign which tells of sharp curves and steep grades for four and a half miles. Fortunately, half that distance is consumed going *down* the tree-covered western slopes. Glimpses of the bright blue waters of Bear Lake are yours during the short descent.

Roll into **Laketown** and enjoy a meal at Kearl's Cafe (no other services). You'll be at the site of the mountain man rendezvous of 1827, where those rough-life solitaries could get their quick fill of companionship and buy goods which had been hauled all the way from Missouri. They paid, on average, a two-thousand-percent hike on St. Louis prices—and often more than that. Flour that went for two cents a pound cost two dollars; coffee rose fifteen cents to two dollars a pound. Diluted alcohol—if you were lucky— went for five dollars a pint. Their currency?—the beaver pelt—at three dollars a pound in 1827, which equalled six dollars an animal if his hide was prime.

Talk was the order of the camp. Stories were swapped of who'd been gun-shot, or caught an arrow in his back, of how one's scars were earned, and how many scalps you'd taken. But one man held all ears that year, for he'd just returned from California. Jedediah Smith spun out tales of West Coast senoritas, of hunger going there and back, of the Mohave Indians who'd fed them on the way out, and the desert-living Diggers (who existed on nuts and roots and insects, and made their clothes of woven grass) whom he met on his return.

And if the stories after a while wore thin, frontier mountain life could be counted on to add new material. As related in a letter written that summer:

[A] party of about 120 Blackfeet approached the camp & killed a Snake Indian and his Squaw. the alarm was immediately given and the Snakes, Utaws whites sallied forth for battle—the enemy fled to the mountains to a small concavity thickly grown with small timber surrounded by open ground. In this engagement the squaws were busily engaged in throwing up batteries and dragging off the dead. There were only six whites engaged in this battle, who immediately advanced within pistol shot and you may be assured that almost every shot counted one. The loss of the Snakes was three killed and the same number wounded; that of the whites, one wounded and two narrowly made their escape; that of the Utaws was none, though they gained great applause for their bravery. The loss of the enemy is not known—six were found dead on the ground. a great number besides were carried off on horses.

Battle statistics were handled less carefully by other participants. Beck-wourth, veteran of many a long evening tale around the campfire (one of Bridger's favorites—"the peetrified forests where peetrified birds sang pee-trified songs, the eight-hour echo that was so useful since you could wind it up by shouting 'Time to get up' when you went to bed''), had soon pumped up the story to "one hundred and seventy-three scalps."

One might wonder why such large parties of Indians often failed to vanquish even small groups of mountain men. Part of the answer lay in armaments. The white man's rifle was deadly at a hundred yards, while the smoothbore musket (traded to the Indians) and the bow could only hit their marks at seventy-five yards or less. Another part of the answer lay in tactics. Indians played percentages; "win-or-die" was the white man's approach to war. If fire from the trappers' guns seemed sure to bring on losses, the warriors saw no slight in waiting for another day. Surprise and stealth were valued as much as mortal bravery.

You've got an easy ten-mile ride to Garden City from Laketown, past great old barns and farmhouses in **Pickleville**, and Sweetwater condominiums by the score. A motorlodge, small market, and a couple of cafes are huddled around the turnoff for Logan. (Campgrounds along the Lake are often full in summer. There's one near Laketown, and two more a mile or so north of Garden City.)

On three rides through this area I've found I like the Lake View Cafe the most. It's just a bit north of the Utah 30/US 89 junction, the food is good and inexpensive, and the people very nice. John Murphy is the owner and cook, and if you twist his arm he'll tell you about his grandfather—a Confederate soldier captured by the North.

And now the climb. **Garden City** sits at almost six thousand feet; the summit less than ten miles east is 7800'. It's rough, but not nearly the worst in Utah. Besides, aspen, evergreen, and cooling breezes are yours when you reach the top. You'll pass many campground turnoffs during the remaining thirty miles to Logan. The canyon is wide at first, then narrows to a pretty gorge that contains a fast-flowing river. An underground spring runs halfway down (near **MP 390**), and offers ice-cold water. Then on to **Logan**, with the picturesque campus of Utah State University, an LDS Temple of stately architecture, and a downtown area with all amenities. (A nice, wide shoulder begins a couple miles or so before town. Ride due west past the University— don't veer onto Canyon Road when you first reach the city limits—and on to Main Street. US 89 drops you into town on 400 North Street.)

Follow 89 south out of Logan to the Utah 165 turnoff for Hyrum, seven miles away. The ride is relatively flat, through an area well-watered by the Little Bear River and mountain runoff. Once at **Hyrum** (cafe, grocery, campground at the nearby reservoir) you can proceed east five miles to 89 again, or take this loop's only spur. (You're in Cache Valley's narrow southern tip. The valley received its name from the practice of trappers burying their furs here for safe keeping—"cacher" in French means "to conceal.")

SPUR A—HARDWARE RANCH—(32 miles roundtrip)

This is a pretty ride, with water and high, steep canyon walls almost all the way. A relatively easy pull (for you're *between* the mountains), it takes you to a nineteen-thousand-acre "game management" ranch where feed is grown for elk. Hundreds of these hungry animals congregate here in winter, and a horse-drawn bobsled escorts you about the grounds. (Try to take the narrow road early in the morning. A campground—open June through October—lies halfway to the ranch.)

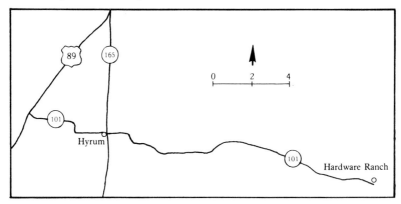

From the Utah 101/US 89 junction it is only sixteen miles to Brigham City. Turn south on 89 and pedal over the low mountain pass separating Cache and Bear River Valleys. You'll ride past the Sherwood Hills Resort (about eleven miles north of Brigham), and then a wonderful sign which says "Downhill Next 8 Miles." During this descent you'll have a pretty view of the Mantua Reservoir (campground), and then a choice of either Utah 90 into **Brigham** (which leads you into town on 200 South Street, next to the Tabernacle), or US 89 to **Ogden**.

(Refer to Chapter Seven for information on the Hwy 89 Brigham City-Ogden stretch.)

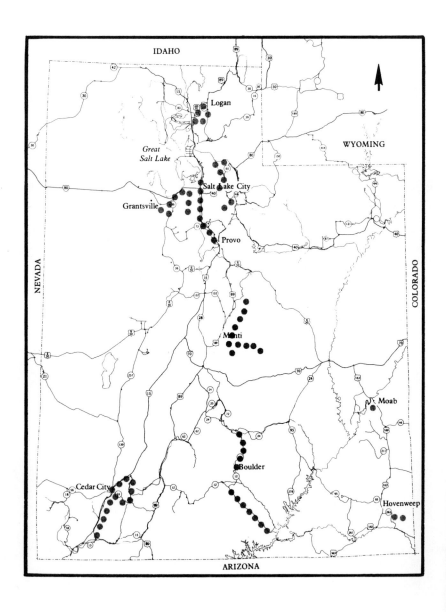

9. WEEKEND RIDES AND OTHER MATTERS

SALT LAKE to PROVO
EAST CANYON—MORGAN—DEVILS SLIDE AREA
SALT LAKE, TOOELE, AND SKULL VALLEYS
BRIGHAM CITY—COLLINSTON—LOGAN
CEDAR CITY—PAROWAN—CEDAR BREAKS
LA VERKIN to CEDAR CITY
MOUNTAIN (ALL TERRAIN) BIKES

The best source of information for short rides in the state is the series of loops and spurs in the preceding chapters. However, there are some short tours which branch off from those already discussed. Therefore, I'll begin with a quick description of these routes, and close with a few suggested trails for mountain bikes.

SALT LAKE to PROVO: 50 miles

This one-hundred-mile roundtrip ride makes an excellent weekend of cycling. The terrain is easy, for you'll cross no mountains, but be prepared for head winds on the way south—especially at the Point of the Mountain. Provo has much to offer, plenty of motels, and a campground (open April through November) at Utah Lake State Park.

There are several acceptable routes from Salt Lake City; your choice will depend upon your point of origin. From the downtown-University region I suggest time-consuming but quiet residential streets to 1300 East and 2100

South, then 1300 East Street south all the way to 10600 South, at the Bell
Canyon Shopping Center. (For those unaccustomed to the numbering system, 1300 East Street is commonly referred to as 13th East, 10600 South as
106th South, et cetera.) Proceed west on 106th South for three blocks then
turn left (south) on 10th East. Ride past Alta High School and follow 10th
East as it curves a bit to run into 9th East. Head south on 9th East several
blocks to the first large intersection. Make a right here and head west on
12300 South. Proceed under Interstate 15 (this is the 124th South Exit, as the
road has curved slightly), turn left (south) on the Frontage Road, and ride
toward the Point of the Mountain.

Some riders prefer the slower traffic along 5th East out of the downtown
area, south to 45th South, then east on that street to 13th East, and then the
route described above. Those who live close to Little Cottonwood Canyon
can ride scenic Dimple Dell Road toward the small community of Draper
and pick up 123rd South there.

Those who live on the west side of Salt Lake have a straight shot south on
Redwood Road (Utah 68) to Bluffdale, where one can either head east to the
I-15 frontage road, or continue south to Utah 73. However, unless you ride
Redwood early on a Saturday morning, or on Sunday, I would choose instead
the very scenic, quiet route of Utah 111. Pick up 111 by riding 3500 South
(Utah 171), 5400 South (Utah 173), or 7800 South (Utah 48—also called
Bingham Highway) west to the Oquirrh Mountains. (Highway 111 is the last
paved north-south road before the mountains, and is great riding all the way
from Magna to Lark.) Continue on 111 as it turns east to run through
Herriman, then on to Redwood Road.

If you have ridden Redwood (68) south to 73, turn east and proceed on 73
to its junction with US 89. For those who have ridden south out of Salt Lake
valley on the frontage road, remain on it past the **State Prison**, past the
Utah 92 turnoff to American Fork Canyon and Timpanogos Cave, and on to
its junction with US 89 just north of Lehi. (89 is called State Street as it runs
past Lehi.) You'll see a sign saying "City Center" with an arrow directing
you (on the appropriately named "Center Street") several blocks west to
downtown **Lehi**. Continue south on 89 past the popular Lehi Cafe, under
I-15, past the junction with Utah 73, and through **American Fork**.

(If you look at Loop Five again you'll find specific information on the
services available in these towns. You'll also notice another option for
approaching American Fork. That is, to head east on Utah 92 from its
junction with the frontage road north of Lehi for seven miles to Utah 74, then
south on 74 to American Fork.)

Remain on US 89 south through **Pleasant Grove**, **Lindon**, and **Orem**,
to the sign at the north edge of **Provo** which directs you east to Brigham
Young University (BYU). Take this or any east-west street south of it to
University Avenue (US 189), and ride University south into the downtown
area. (If University Avenue is too busy, ride south on 100 East Street.)

I suggest the University Avenue approach because it takes you through the older "heart" of the city. Continue south to Center Street and you'll be near the beautiful old Tabernacle and the City and County Building. Ride west on Center Street to the delightful mall area of tiny shops and restaurants, then back north on 500 West Street (the in-town designation for US 89). This way you'll pass the St. Francis Catholic Church—which may remind you of the Dominguez-Escalante trail through this area—and the Pioneer Village between 500 and 600 North.

Provo has much to offer in the way of museums (on *and* off the BYU campus) and historic homes. Its distance from Salt Lake makes it a perfect place for an early morning Saturday ride, a motel room and long walks around town, and a leisurely pedal home on Sunday.

You might alter your return route by riding Center Street (Utah 114) west across the interstate, then north to Pleasant Grove. (Follow the signs just south of Lakeview to Utah Lake State Park, which has a campground.) When you reach US 89 jag south on it for about a quarter-mile, then turn left (north) on Utah 146. Continue north about six miles to Utah 92 (American Fork Canyon), then head west to the I-15 frontage road.

EAST CANYON—MORGAN—DEVILS SLIDE AREA

The great number of route alternatives in this area enables you to choose a short or longer loop, or an out-and-back ride of any length over the same terrain. Difficulty of pedalling can also be tailored to individual wishes; the ride is quite easy if you avoid the Porterville to East Canyon Reservoir run (it's uphill in that direction), and the East Canyon Reservoir to Henefer stretch in *either* direction.

From Ogden, one heads south out of town on Washington Boulevard (US 89), or Harrison Boulevard (Utah 203) to its junction with 89, then south on 89 to Interstate 84, and the interstate shoulder to the Mountain Green exit (**#92**). This route is especially handy for those who live in Ogden and would like to camp at East Canyon Reservoir (or plug into the other sights along Loop Six).

For an easy point of reference, I will assume you are either driving or riding from Salt Lake to East Canyon Reservoir. (Refer to Loop Six for the necessary route information.) From the campground there, ride north seven and a half miles on Utah 66 to **Porterville**. It is a very pretty downhill run, past the dam along East Canyon Creek. When you get to Porterville (no services) you have the choice to continue on 66 to Morgan, or ride the far less travelled side road through Richville, Littleton, Milton, and Peterson. If you choose the latter route, make a left at the only intersection in Porterville, ride up a steep hill, and follow the road as it turns north past the 1895 Porterville Ward Meeting House (now a private residence).

This unnumbered side route (the Richville-Littleton road) is my choice by far, not only because it has almost no traffic, but because it is high on the mountain benches, providing a great view of the valley. There are no services in these tiny towns until Pendleton's Country Store in **Peterson** (groceries, ice cream, drinks).

Cross under I-84, and make a right on the small road which runs back to Morgan, or go left to **Mountain Green** (no services) on the side road, then take the interstate shoulder to US 89, and go north on 89 to **Ogden**. (From Ogden you can wind your way back to Salt Lake; directions provided in Loop Seven.) However, if you choose to ride back to Morgan, you'll travel through **Enterprise**, past nice farm country and dairy herds, and on to **Stoddard**. Here you'll find the Stoddard Inn, open seven days a week (serves breakfast at 7 A.M.) with everything from hamburgers and cold beer to steak and shrimp.

Continue riding east on the side road and you'll come to the turnoff for **Morgan** (grocery, cafes), which if taken will then lead you south to **Porter-ville** once again. Or, continue east past the Morgan turnoff to another cafe only a half-mile or so further (called the Hitching Post), and follow the road as it turns south to run beneath the interstate. You'll come to a "T": a right turn takes you back to the original turnoff road for Morgan; a left turn takes you one-half mile to Como Springs.

Como Springs, a 1950s-style resort, is a relic of the past. A secluded spot open only during the summer, it has a swimming pool (the mineral water is 80°, but is cooled by the wind), campground, bar, grilled food, wooden roller rink, and motel. A road just south of the Recreation Area runs due east three miles to a golf course, and ends. If this road is taken west it comes out in Morgan at 100 South Street and State (Utah 66).

You can make this a larger loop still by proceeding east on I-84 from Morgan (no side road available) about eight miles to the giant chute-like rock formation called **Devils Slide**. (Three miles before this, at Exit 108, is a place called Taggarts. It looks like a small gas station, but serves hamburgers as well.) Take Exit 111 just past Devils Slide and cross under I-84 toward the town of **Croydon** (no services). A paved road runs north out of town for almost three miles toward the distant Lost Creek State Park, and though you'd need a mountain bike to get there, the first paved section provides such a nice view of fields and mountains that it's well worth the effort.

Finally, return to Croydon and head south to the historical marker on Weber Canyon described in Loop Six. At this point you can cross the interstate to Henefer and proceed south on Utah 65 to East Canyon Reservoir, or ride on to Echo Junction. (Pick up the route from there in Chapter Six.)

SALT LAKE, TOOELE, AND SKULL VALLEYS

I've already mentioned various routes through and around Salt Lake, including the best roads to travel out of the city in all directions. However, there are some additional areas in the city, and the valleys just west of Salt Lake (to the Stansbury Mountains) which justify specific discussion.

A. *West Side (Salt Lake, Bingham Canyon, to the Stansbury Mountains)*

In the discussion above on the Salt Lake to Provo run I mentioned the lovely riding available on Utah 111—from Magna south to Lark. This is gently rolling terrain, and provides a good view of Salt Lake against the Wasatch Mountains, as well as proximity to the Oquirrhs. One of the prettiest sights, though one would not expect it, is the many-colored east side of the Bingham open-pit copper mine (largest in North America). This can be reached by riding west on Utah 48 (Bingham Highway) through the well-kept little town of **Copperton** (two cafes, and a beautiful school building), and past a small museum to the mine road entrance.

Next to the museum is a historical marker which tells of the fascinating history of this area. Once used for cattle grazing and timber, this mineral-rich canyon became the home of an incorporated city of three thousand people. The marker mentions the following nationalities as mine laborers: Greeks, Italians, Armenians, Mexicans, Japanese, Chinese, British, and Austrians. But the names given the old groupings of wooden houses up this canyon tell the same story—Greek Town, Frog Town, Wop Town, Jap Town...

Sunday morning is the best time to visit this area, but even then a cyclist may be refused admittance to the mine overlook point. The final two-mile climb—over gravel, dirt, and a partially paved road—is rough. The company has informed me that one can call ahead (322-7510, or 322-7511) to see if on a particular day you will be allowed access. Unfortunately, all the old homes in this canyon, and the city of Bingham itself, have been consumed by the expanding pit. A couple of the old houses remain, but are off-limits to the public, and beyond view from the road.

Utah 111 can be ridden north to **Magna**, then to the intersection with Utah 201 (the western extension of 2100 South). Turn left on 201 and head west for three miles to the Utah 202 turnoff. Ride northwest on it for two and a half miles to **Great Salt Lake State Park** (campground, swimming, showers), and the newly rebuilt Saltair Resort. (Both the park and resort are currently under water.) Continue west on the shoulder of I-80 for two miles to the Tooele exit.

Most residents of Salt Lake seldom travel to the two valleys immediately west—Rush Valley, between the Oquirrh and Stansbury Mountains, and Skull Valley, between the Stansbury and Cedar Mountain ranges. Both areas, however, make for excellent, relatively level riding. There's little traffic, many communities with cafes and motels, and campgrounds in the eleven-thousand-foot Stansburys (as pine and aspen filled as the Wasatch, and *far* less crowded).

From the I-80 turnoff it's only thirteen miles south to **Tooele** (all amenities), and another fourteen miles south to a link-up with Loop Five. From here you can continue south four miles to Utah 199, then west to Utah 138 which leads north to the Stansbury campgrounds and **Grantsville**, or further west over Johnsons Pass to **Dugway Proving Grounds** (no services). Once at the Dugway entrance one can turn north and ride through Skull Valley (and the Gosiute Indian Reservation), then past the old site of Iosepa (see Loop Seven), and back to I-80.

Grantsville (cafe, grocery, and two motels) was once called "Twenty Wells" because of the springs there. The Donner Party in 1846 rested at the Grantsville site, looped around the north end of the Stansburys, returned south to the springs at Iosepa, and then began the trek to Pilot Peak.

B. *City Creek Canyon*

This controlled-access area is open to cyclists on odd-numbered days. It's a beautiful undeveloped canyon which climbs almost six miles to more than six thousand feet elevation (ending in a lovely park area, enclosed by steep mountains, evergreens, and an ice-cold creek). The road is off-limits to cars on the days when bikes are allowed, but don't assume you've got the pavement to yourself. Joggers have been nailed by cyclists screaming around the many blind curves, and workers at the Water Treatment Plant drive their vehicles even on bike days.

In the past, bikers were allowed on the road anytime between deer season and Memorial Day, since the canyon was closed to cars for those months. But the policy has changed twice in the last five years; be sure to call ahead (535-7911).

You can reach the canyon mouth by riding north through Memory Grove from downtown, by climbing through the Avenues to the intersection of B Street and 11th Avenue and heading north down the hill, and by riding north on the road on the east side of the Capitol Building (Capitol Bonneville Boulevard).

C. *Mill Creek Canyon*

This is a non-controlled access, six-mile-long canyon running east into the Wasatch. While it is not very steep, it is, like City Creek, almost a constant uphill grade. The Log Haven Restaurant—a couple of miles up—is a great place for Sunday brunch. Try to avoid this road on Saturday afternoons, especially in summer.

Mill Creek Canyon begins just east of the intersection of Wasatch Boulevard and 3800 South State Street. There are several restaurants in nearby Olympus Hills shopping center (Wasatch Blvd. and 3900 South).

D. *Big and Little Cottonwood Canyons*

I strongly suggest that bikers avoid these very busy, narrow canyons. The same scenery is available—at far less risk—in many other places nearby, and in countless other spots throughout the state.

BRIGHAM CITY—COLLINSTON—LOGAN—
BRIGHAM CITY—65 miles

This short tour is an attractive, relatively easy (if travelled clockwise—only a few rough pulls) loop around the 9500′ Wellsville Mountains. Refer to Chapters Seven and Eight for historical and service information on the areas and larger towns.

Ride north out of **Brigham City** on Utah 69 through **Honeyville** (general store) to **Crystal Springs Resort** (swimming, campground, snack bar) a couple of miles north of town. Continue north to **Deweyville** (no services), over a low pass into Cache Valley (Bear River has cut a lovely gorge north of the road) on Utah 30. At the Utah 25 junction you can shave seven miles off the loop by turning south, and meeting US 89 just east of the town of **Wellsville** (cafe). Or, continue east eight miles on Utah 30 to **Logan**, and return to Brigham City on US 89. (Refer to Chapter Eight for information on the Logan to Brigham City stretch.)

CEDAR CITY—PAROWAN—CEDAR BREAKS— CEDAR CITY—60 miles

This is a dandy, scenic ride, with only one climb—four thousand feet over fifteen miles! In fact, the sign says it's a thirteen percent grade in places. If you like your knees as they are try this tiny loop in the other direction—Cedar City to Cedar Breaks (see Loop Three for information), then to Parowan and back to the beginning. But if you're part mountain goat, or just like tackling real beasts now and then, give it a shot.

Ride Main Street north out of **Cedar City** and under Interstate 15. Make a right at the Alpine Lanes Bowling Alley and proceed northeast on this interstate-paralleling side road for nine miles to a Husky truck stop. At this point the road crosses I-15 to the little town of **Summit** (no services), then winds on for eight miles more to **Parowan** (all amenities; review history of this town and area in Chapter Three).

Signs in the downtown area direct you south out of town on Utah 143 to Brian Head Ski Resort and Cedar Breaks. The tough climb takes you through a beautiful alpine area, but the road is dangerously narrow. (Most bikers weave a bit on especially steep grades; train yourself to avoid this hazardous riding flaw. And pull this hill early in the day, before too much traffic appears.) It's fifteen mile to **Brian Head** Ski Resort (restaurants, grocery, motel), and about seven miles beyond that to the **Cedar Breaks** National Monument Visitor Center.

LA VERKIN to CEDAR CITY—47 miles

You may recall that during the discussion of Loop Three, when we left Zion National Park heading west and reached the junction of Utah Hwys 15/17 just north of La Verkin, I mentioned an alternate route which would cut the loop in half. This almost straight shot is that cutoff, and also makes for an excellent weekend ride south out of Cedar City, or a fast approach to both sections of Zion.

From the Utah 15/17 junction, turn right and pedal north for eight miles to I-15. The road is narrow and hilly, and you'll ride through the tidy community of **Toquerville** (no services, but several well-preserved nineteenth-century buildings of architectural interest). At the junction of I-15 and Utah 17 there is an old bandshell and cement floor, surrounded by a fence. This is the once-popular open-air "Starlite Dancing" local hot spot.

A small side road next to the bandshell proceeds along the east side of the interstate for one mile, and then comes to an abrupt end. I lifted my heavily laden touring bike over the fence and bushwhacked to the interstate, but you can save yourself the trouble by merely riding the interstate shoulder north, taking the Browse exit (**MP 30+**), and riding the frontage road (east side of I-15) north for a mile, where you'll come to a "Dead End" sign and an access point (Exit 31) to the interstate. (I'm sure your eye will catch the frontage road extension north on the *west* side of I-15 at this point; but don't bother with it. I've tried *both* sides of *every* exit along this stretch. In this case the west side road is gravel only.)

From Exit 31 you have no alternative to interstate travel for about five miles or so—to the Black Ridge exit. Take it and follow the road beneath the interstate to the west side, then north (following the sign) to Ash Creek Reservoir. (You'll have splendid scenery from the interstate, and occasionally what looks like a Midwest fishing hole. Expect to run into cattle on this pretty ride.) Continue north about three miles after the reservoir to a point where the road runs beneath the interstate again. Follow it to the east side of I-15 and the entrance to the fantastic landforms of Zion National Park—Kolob Section (no campground). A very rough five-mile climb to the end-of-road observation point is well worth the trouble. Catch your breath, rest your legs, and study the 150-million-year-old sandstone before you.

North of the Park you must ride the interstate for another mile, then take **Exit 42** and proceed on side roads all the way to Cedar City. The town of **Kanarraville** has a campground, a small market with hot sandwiches, and the Ranch Steak House (reportedly a favorite of Robert Redford's). This is very pretty, level riding; you're between the tree- and sage-covered Cedar and Harmony Mountains, and entering the southern tip of Cedar Valley. Follow the road as it runs to the west side of I-15 again, then crosses for the last time and takes you into **Cedar City** at the Arco Station. You are on the southernmost extension of Main Street; make a right and pedal north into downtown.

MOUNTAIN (ALL-TERRAIN) BIKES

The mountain bike rider in this state has every kind of terrain available, and some of the prettiest scenery in the nation. It is to be hoped that he will realize the danger such bikes pose to some environments, and not spark the kind of negative reaction already present in Colorado. The dirt and gravel roads which we've avoided in our loops become accessible, and no one will argue against mountain bikes in such areas. You can follow the Pony Express, Hole-in-the-Rock, and other trails, pedal the slickrock on a designated route outside Moab, and ride unpaved mountain roads to mountain summits. Simply use this rule of thumb to avoid antagonism: if you, as a cyclist, wouldn't like to see a motorized dirt bike scarring a landscape, then don't take a mountain bike there. Sure, you won't do as much damage. But a thousand other bikers might follow your example.

Remember that mountain bikes are completely excluded from Wilderness Areas, from National Parks (except on roads and those paths specifically marked "bike path"), and from National Forests (except roads and those areas specified as "Multiple Use").

The following are a few of the many excellent mountain bike rides and tours in Utah.

A. *Moab Slickrock Trail*—12 miles (roundtrip)

This twelve-mile beauty takes in some spectacular southern Utah sights, and has a painted line of white dashes across the rock to allow you to pick up great speed, while not worrying that you'll fly over a precipice. (It was actually created for motorcyclists.) Stop in the Rim Cyclery bike shop (94 West/1st North 259-5333), the local travel council (805 N. Main 259-8825), or the Canyonlands National Park Service office (446 South Main Street 259-7164) for directions and information on other back-country rides and trail conditions. While at Rim Cyclery, pick up a copy of Todd Campbell's short book on other mountain bike rides near Moab.

B. *Capitol Reef*—130 miles (roundtrip)

This is one of the best rides around, with pavement for fifty miles, two- and four-wheel jeep roads for the remaining eighty. And not a single mile passes that isn't different from the one before. From the snow-covered Henry and Boulder Mountains, to Navajo, Kayenta, and Wingate sandstone walls, to the brilliant colors of Long Canyon and desert valleys filled with chaparral, your eyes will tire even sooner than your legs.

Begin with a ride along "Scenic Drive" from the Visitor Center to nearby Capitol Gorge, then pedal Utah 24 east out of the park. Just beyond the park boundary you'll see the hard-packed dirt and gravel Notom Road heading south up a hill. (Expect soft sand in places, especially along creekbeds; these areas can be difficult, but are not long.) This is your route—thirty-five miles south to the Burr Trail Road, then west thirty-six more to Boulder. But be prepared. There are no services along the way, and water (present in pools and potholes and an occasional creek when I made the ride in January) must be purified. Call or write ahead to determine availability of water, or convince a jeep-equipped friend to meet you each night in camp.

Once in Boulder you have all services available, then the beautiful paved road north to Utah 24 and the final leg east to the Visitor Center.
Superintendent
Capitol Reef National Park
Torrey, Utah 84775
(801) 425-3871

C. *Hovenweep National Monument*—16 miles (one-way)

This ride—at the southeast corner of Loop Two—is one I had to forego due to road conditions. With a mountain bike you can negotiate the last sixteen miles to the Anasazi ruins. (There is a campground at the northern ruin site.)

D. *Skyline Drive*—100 miles (one-way)

This one-hundred-mile dirt road (which parallels US 89 from Fairview to Manti) is spectacular in fall. Access is available from any of the towns along the southeast arm of Loop Five.

E. *Guardsman Pass*—12 miles (one-way)

This approximately twelve-mile run among the mountaintops features great views of Heber Valley and Mount Timpanogos. Begin the ride a half-mile south of Brighton—on the paved road which curls up the mountainside to the east. You'll at last come to a junction; the dirt road south leads down the mountain to Midway and Heber. Make a left instead and proceed north to Park City. You'll come out one block east of downtown.

F. *Hole-in-the-Rock*—55 miles (one-way)

This fantastic run begins about six miles east of Escalante, and angles southeasterly to the Colorado River. The first half of the trail is hard-packed earth in most places, with the majestic Straight Cliffs and green shadscale for scenery. While relatively level, there are sufficient hills and sandy washes to instruct the neophyte in mountain biking.

But the second half is another story. One of the pioneers wrote:

> It's the roughest country you or anybody else ever seen; it's nothing in the world but rocks and holes, hills and hollows. The mountains are just one solid rock as smooth as an apple.

And so it remains a century later; a land of steep grades, dry washes, slickrock, and gorgeous scenery. (Two vehicles were involved in caching food and water for us, and both broke down. But the three mountain bikes—each carrying forty-five pounds of gear—took the rough terrain in stride.)

You'll find the only water available at "Willow Tank," a bit beyond the halfway point and two miles before Dance Hall Rock. A biker could make the trip by starting off with two gallons (I managed to mount eight water bottles in my panniers), and riding to Willow Tank the first day. Water from that source will take you to the Hole, which is a rough 1000-foot, boulder-strewn descent to the Colorado. (See Loop Three for the history of this trek.) I used purification tablets to drink the river water (though I now carry and much prefer the pump action, inexpensive, lightweight, fast-working water purifiers); a biker would have to pack a large quantity—enough to get him back to Willow Tank—up the Hole.

Whatever you decide on provisions, don't count on passing motorists to render assistance. I didn't even *see* a vehicle for two days. Good luck.

G. *White Rim Trail*—117 miles (roundtrip)

This is the granddaddy of the southern Utah offroad tours, the one that is quickly gaining a reputation as THE mountain bike ride of the West. And without taking anything away from the beauty and thrills of other tours, I must agree. You won't be pedalling snow-covered mountain peaks or aspen forests, but you'll be dazzled by red rock scenery and fantastic geologic formations.

These are purchased at a cost, however. Expect no services, no safe water until purified, and at some times of the year no water, period. Call or write to the national park ranger station in Moab to check on recent rainfall and road conditions, and ask them to send you a Canyonlands park map and the pamphlet "Guide to the White Rim Trail."

To reach the White Rim, travel north out of Moab on US 163 eleven miles to the Utah 313 turnoff. Turn west. This is the road that goes to Dead Horse Point, but instead of following the signs to the Visitor Center and Dead Horse Point Overlook, you will head for the Island in the Sky ranger station. (Don't worry, signs will lead the way. Besides, there aren't many roads in these parts, and the ranger station sits on the only other paved road in this section of the park.) Talk to the rangers, heed their warnings, and sign in. I travelled in the near waterless month of October, and several times was very happy I had noted on my map where the rangers told me I might find water.

You will be fighting soft sand and tough hills for many miles, but the scenery is beyond compare. (The 117 roundtrip mileage figure comes from my computations of parking near the ranger station and then returning on Utah 313 to the Mineral Canyon turnoff. Without this additional leg of the journey the distance is around 100 miles.) I suggest traveling this loop counterclockwise, as this leaves the enormous climb up the switchbacked Shafer Trail for the end. Sure it's a bear, especially if taken when one is tired from the effort of pedaling over tough roads for two or three days. But Shafer is a fitting, memorable end to this rough ride.

H. *Navajo Lake/Zion Park/Kolob Terrace*—138 miles (roundtrip)

This fantastic ride includes the alpine beauty of Navajo Lake, the amazing geology and color of Zion National Park, tough climbs to the sculpted sandstone of Kolob Terrace, and a final long ascent from lowland sage to the pine and fir surroundings of Dixie National Forest. I did this trip in two days, and wish I'd had the time and sense to plan on twice that long. Once again water is a problem, even if you take the ride in the cool days and cold nights of fall. Your body must make a tremendous effort to negotiate these rough miles; make sure to saddlebag plenty of food and water, and take a purifier.

I began at the Duckcreek Field Ranger Station near Navajo Lake, pedalled the 37 miles south to Utah 9 (all but the first five or so unpaved), then turned west and entered Zion Park. (Read the notes on riding Zion's tunnels in Chapter Three.) Turn north on Kolob Road once you reach Virgin, for fifteen or so miles of pavement, another thirty-five of dirt, some tough climbs and rough riding and wonderful scenery. You'll come out on Utah 14 with Cedar City only five miles west, and eastward a long climb of thirteen miles to the summit. The road tops out at the turnoff for Cedar Breaks (only three miles north), and then comes the easy, top-of-the-mountain alpine riding all of us adore. From the turnoff on to Navajo Lake is another 7½ miles.

I. *Panguitch Lake/Parowan/Brian Head*—70 miles (roundtrip)

This beautiful Dixie National Forest loop combines Utah's highest town (9700') with long views of desert valleys. Water is a problem only if what you carry can't get you thirty unpaved miles downhill, or up a paved road climb that qualifies for one of the roughest in Utah—thirteen miles at a thirteen-percent grade.

I parked my car at the friendly Rustic Lodge on the west side of Panguitch Lake, pedalled the North Shore Road to the first major turnoff (dirt) north, and followed it through Horse Valley and past Red Creek Reservoir to Paragonah. (If you have the time don't miss the rough four-wheel jeep road ride to Kings Valley on the way.) You'll have pavement all the way from that point to the all-services town of Parowan, up the giant hill to Brian Head (stop in the bike shop there for directions to more nearby mountain bike rides), and then the final sixteen miles back to Panguitch Lake.

One word of caution: if you are crazy enough to do this in a single day, as I did, pack a light. Luckily a full October moon illuminated the road sufficiently for me to negotiate the final miles. I passed at least a dozen mule deer too close for comfort, and shouted as I neared them to clear the road. Travel light and spend the night at a Parowan or Brian Head motel, or gear up and camp along the way. Don't be as silly as I was.

J. *Moki Dugway/Valley of the Gods/Goosenecks*—40 miles (roundtrip)

Park a car at the top of Moki Dugway (30 miles south of Natural Bridges National Monument, on Utah 261), take the short dirt-road ride out to Muley Point for a view of Arizona, then swallow hard and head downhill. You'll drop a thousand feet during three miles of switchbacks, and love every minute of it.

Make a left (east) at the bottom to ride the sixteen miles of sometimes dirt road through Valley of the Gods, a well-named expanse with huge rock forms towering from the desert floor. They take on eerie, godlike forms if viewed at dawn or dusk.

You'll come out on US 163. Turn right (southwest) and pedal the easy four miles to the paved road turnoff back toward Moki Dugway. A mile later you will see Utah 316, and a sign for the Goosenecks of the San Juan. Make the ride, even if you're tired. The view will revitalize you.

Start early if you plan to do this in a single day, for climbing the Moki Dugway will take you far longer than did the descent. Or make it a perfect weekend ride, by camping out along the way or adding a few miles to sleep inside in Mexican Hat. The little town has two motels, and the finest Navajo frybread that I've ever tasted.

Utah is blessed with far too many mountain bike roads and trails to include here. I suggest you get into the habit of hitting the area bike and mountaineering shops, for information on the best routes in that region. Supplement those directions with topo maps and your backcountry touring kit, *and* far more food and water than the maps tell you you'll need.

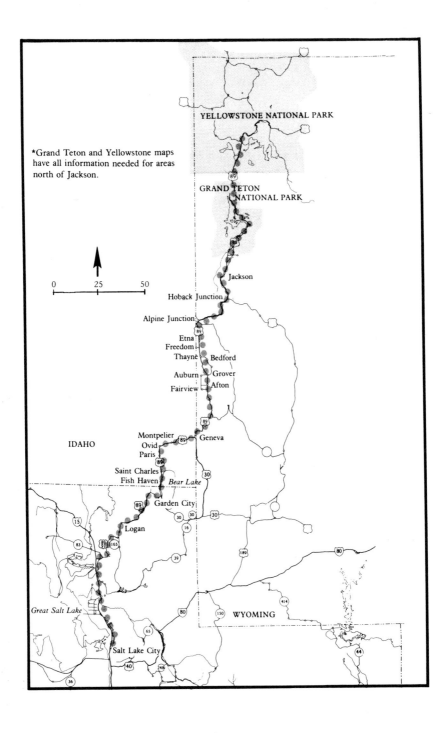

*Grand Teton and Yellowstone maps
have all information needed for areas
north of Jackson.

10. THE GRAND TETONS AND YELLOWSTONE LOOP

SALT LAKE—BRIGHAM CITY—

MONTPELIER (IDAHO)—

JACKSON (WYOMING)—

YELLOWSTONE PARK (south entrance)

Mileage: 350

Mountain lakes, deep pine and fir forests, raging ice-cold rivers, historic trails and battle sites, one of the prettiest mountain ranges in the world, and the animals and thermal wonders of our first national park—all are here for the cyclist who can handle a few rough mountain passes, including a climb over the Continental Divide. The tour seems tailormade for a two week vacation. Seven fifty-mile days take you to Yellowstone's southern entrance; the second week is left for geysers and mud pots.

Late May through early October is the only time for travel in this high mountain region. But summer has its problems—the thousands of motorized tourists who make the trek. The best weeks for riding in the Park are before Memorial Day and after Labor Day. You'll face cool weather at these times, but empty campgrounds, more animals, and fewer cars make it preferable.

There are, however, ways to avoid the congestion even if you can't travel at the suggested times. I've made this ride twice, and eventually found a far less hectic route through Yellowstone—especially if you ride early in the day.

But don't think the parks are all there is to see on this tour. The route from Logan north takes you past lakes, rivers, and reservoirs, through alpine scenery and mountain canyons, always with services nearby.

If you begin this tour in Salt Lake, consult Chapters Seven and Eight for information on the ride to Bear Lake. Some people however prefer to pedal through less populated areas, and start off from a point further north. You can drive or take a bus to **Logan,** and start your trek with a pretty forty-mile canyon ride. Drop down to Bear Lake at **Garden City,** and head north.

The thirty miles of level riding on US 89 from Garden City to Montpelier is a very pleasant, scenic entrance into Idaho. The highway follows Bear Lake's western shore (see Chapter Eight for a discussion of the 1827 mountain man rendezvous and Indian battle there), through many little towns with interesting histories and attractive nineteenth-century architecture. You'll ride past two campgrounds a mile north of Garden City on the way to **Fish Haven**—named thus because two men in 1864 "threw a seine ... and brought out 96 large trout." There are two general stores, and beautiful views of Bear Lake, with yellow-flowered meadows on the west, and rolling green hills of sage and juniper behind.

US 89 along this stretch has a nice shoulder as it runs through **St. Charles** (grocery, and a drive-in on the north edge of town), **Bloomington** (no services), and **Paris** (all amenities, plus a Tabernacle built in 1888—free tours are given to the public). **Ovid** has a small grocery (closed on Sundays), and lies only six miles from a good-sized town, **Montpelier** (all amenities). You'll cross Bear River on your approach, and if it's early summer when you pedal by you'll see scores of carp spawning in the bulrushes.

US 89 runs through Montpelier to a junction with US 30 on the east edge of town. Turn north at this point, ride past the motels and supermarkets for less than a mile, then make a right (at the City Park) as 89 continues east up Montpelier Canyon. (Be sure to stock up on food in Montpelier, for you've got two mountain passes before another grocery.) Several campgrounds sit along the road as you begin your climb; a KOA is first, then public campgrounds beginning just before **MP 30.** This is a lovely ride, and not too tough a pull to the summit of 6938'. You eventually drop out of the trees into a small watered valley; and the little town of **Geneva** (no services) comes at **MP 40+.**

On my 1976 ride to Yellowstone I stopped at a small grocery/post office in town. The people were extremely nice, and as I munched a candy bar they told me of their town and valley. On my second trip to Old Faithful, in 1983, I'd hoped to talk with these good folks again. But the store had closed, and I had to ride another four miles for a meal and conversation. 89 turns north along a range of hills, providing a good look at the green, fertile valley, and white-topped mountain ranges in the distance. The raucous calls of magpies will escort you out of Idaho, and across the Wyoming line.

If you pedal this stretch on Thursday through Sunday (the restaurant is closed the rest of the week) you'll have an opportunity to meet a grand lady at the Canyon Inn. Just across the border, this restaurant-bar-motel opens late in the afternoon, and serves the best Mexican food I've tasted north of Santa Fe. But the real treat is the bar tenderness, a woman whose half-century of life has left her tough, but kind. For twenty-six years Athy Long tended bar all around the world, in clubs on military bases. For a while she worked in a factory making beer bottles in Waco, Texas, and later stripped caviar in Soda Springs. With all those miles behind her what she wanted most was to come home to the mountains. Now she greets Japanese tourists in their native language, with a straight face warns New Yorkers driving to watch for "jackalopes" ("They'll sure-nuf put a hole in the *best* tire!"), talks Swiss tourists into yodelling, and laughs at the French who "take pictures of the pictures." I watched her in action one night until 1:00 A.M., as she turned a thirty-minute rest stop for Park-bound folks into a memorable experience.

It's forty-three miles from the restaurant to Afton, the first twelve miles a beautiful climb up Salt River Canyon (campground at **MP 64**; summit of 7630' at **MP 68+**). Work was being done in 1983 to make the road a little straighter, but even then the switchbacks weren't extremely steep. Once you're down the other side you'll have gently rolling hills through the southern tip of fertile Star Valley, often referred to as the "Little Switzerland of America" due to its "gently sloping valley floor . . . dotted with neat farms surrounded by steep, rugged mountains." Dairies are the valley's principal industry, and when you pedal into Afton beneath the elkhorn arch you'll have your choice of several cheese shops.

Afton is a pleasant town, with motels, cafes, a grocery and a beautiful canyon (Swift Creek) only a quarter-mile from Main Street. Proceed through town to a brown sign pointing east for the "Periodic Spring." The sign is on Second Avenue; ride this to the canyon mouth, where the road becomes hard-packed dirt. A campground lies one mile east, and a small reservoir good for fishing.

Return and ride north out of Afton on US 89, over the slight ridge which forms the northern border of Star Valley. The town of **Grover** has a small natural foods store; **Thayne** houses a huge Swiss Cheese Factory (with restaurant); and **Etna** has a cafe and motel. Then it's eleven pretty miles along Salt River and Palisades Reservoir (home of pelicans and cranes) to the town of **Alpine Junction** (motels, cafes, grocery).

Three rivers meet at Alpine Junction—the Snake, Salt, and Greys. (You'll be following the first of these all the way to Yellowstone.) I spent a long evening in 1983 with the owner of the bakery and bar on the north side of the Snake, the same gentleman who lives in the nearby large white Greek Revival–style home. We talked of his intended creation—a *completely* planned community on this site—a town which will be European in flavor, and the opposite of the unstructured and wildly developed Alpine Junction (which lies on the south side of the river).

The twenty-three miles from Alpine to Hoback Junction is one of the prettiest legs of the entire trip. This region is called the "Grand Canyon" of the Snake, for the cold waters flow through a deep gorge between snow-capped mountains. Occasional waterfalls are seen, as are cranes, hawks, deer, and even moose. (Always be cautious around wild animals—*especially* when their young are nearby.) But while you're enjoying all the scenery don't forget to watch the road for rocks, which sometimes fall from high, sheer cliffs above.

Astoria Hot Springs (**MP 138+**) is a large commercial campground with snackbar, swimming, laundry facilities, et cetera. Three miles further (**MP 141**) is **Hoback Junction**, which has a motel (open May through November), two general stores, and a great old-time ice cream fountain. From this point to Jackson (13 miles north) there is again the pretty Snake, the tree-covered hills, and a range of high mountains in the distance. A fertile valley lies between the road and the river, and giant hay bales—the size of houses and shaped like loaves of bread—sit in the fields.

The busy tourist town of **Jackson Hole** is a pleasant shock after all the tranquil miles, and has bike shops, motels, a nearby campground (Rising Sage Campground—with indoor pool and sauna, pack horses, chuckwagon breakfasts and dinners—two miles north of town on 89), great eating places (my favorite is the quiet "Alice's Restaurant"), and an information center on the north side. Helicopter rides and thrilling Snake River float trips are also available.

In the small town square stands a monument to "the first white man in Wyoming," who passed this way on a trip which included the discovery of Yellowstone Park. The man was John Colter, a former member of the Lewis and Clark Expedition. His path through Jackson Hole—this glacial-scarred valley surrounded by the Gros Ventre, Hoback and Teton Mountains—was followed by so many other trappers that it became a crossroads of the fur trade. Named Jackson's Hole in 1829 after mountain man David E. Jackson, it was once the home of many beaver streams. Today a huge elk refuge and **Grand Teton National Park** prohibit development.

Follow US 89 north out of town, up the long grade which rewards you with one of the most majestic sights in the West—the Tetons. (Early French-Canadian trappers first saw the mountains from the west. Three peaks jutted into the sky, and brought about the name of "Trois Tetons"—three breasts.") These snow-covered, jagged pinnacles are especially beautiful when viewed across the sparkling blue of the Park's many lakes. Thirteen miles north of Jackson is the Visitor Center, Moose Entrance Station, and turnoff for the Teton Park Road—a path much closer to the lakes and campsites through this area. (Campgrounds are present at South Jenny Lake Junction, Signal Mountain, Colter Bay Village, and Lizard Creek; lodging is available at Jenny Lake, Signal Mountain and Jackson Lake. There are cafes or stores with food at all sites mentioned—except for Lizard Creek—plus the Moose Entrance Station.)

Take your time in seeing this magnificent area. There are many hiking trails which take you to pristine lakes, past moose and mule deer, into lovely meadows of wildflowers, and up mountainsides to never-melting glaciers. The Park map which you'll receive upon entering will show you the trails. Good fishing, swimming, boating, and horseback rides are also available. But remember that this is high mountain country; the summer season is short. Park brochures warn of occasional snow as late as June, and many facilities are closed from late September to mid-May.

Forty miles north of the Moose Entrance Station you'll ride out of Grand Teton National Park. There are seven attractive miles of pedalling to the edge of Yellowstone. **Flagg Ranch Village** (cafe, grocery, campground) lies along this stretch, as does the **Huckleberry Hot Spring** (campground, grocery) one mile off the main road. And then, at last, you've reached **Yellowstone National Park.**

The name of our nation's first national park is one of antiquity—applied by the Indians to the river which begins here, and flows through grand canyons of distinct yellow coloration. But most Indians found this snow-swept area too inhospitable for residence, and travel was usually easier around the present park. (Those small bands which did come through refrained from crossing dense forests, remaining instead near Yellowstone River, or the Great Bannock Trail—and thereby missing most or all geyser areas. The rising steam, viewed from a distance, brought about the name "Burning Mountains.") In fact, even the poor Sheepeater Indians—the only permanent occupants of the region—knew little of the area. Five Sheepeaters were employed as guides by General Sheridan (of Civil War fame) during his 1882 exploration, who wrote that upon viewing the geyser basin, the Indians "exhibited more astonishment and wonder than any of us." And when the Nez Perce crossed the area during their retreat from the U. S. Army, they had to force a white man to act as guide.

People refused to believe the stories Colter and Jim Bridger told of the various wonders, and the latter responded by stretching the truth a bit. When a hearer cocked an eye at the truthful report of Obsidian Cliff—a giant hill of volcanic glass just south of Mammoth Hot Springs—he built it into a transparent mountain which acted as a telescopic lens. Through it, he claimed, one could easily view elk feeding peaceably twenty-five miles away. And when his tale of boiling pools brought disbelieving stares, he told of catching trout in the colder waters below, then pulling the fish so slowly through the boiling upper layers that his dinner was cooked on the way out.

The Park has many stories. From the 1870 Washburn-Doane Expedition (on which a man named Everts became separated from his group, lost his horse, and spent a frightening thirty-seven days alone in the wilds); to the five stagecoach holdups within Park boundaries; to the building of the massive log and stone Old Faithful Inn in 1904.

The first time I rode to Yellowstone I managed to do everything wrong. I hit Jackson on the insanely busy July 4th holiday, then scheduled myself an eighty-mile day from Jenny Lake to Old Faithful. I left late enough in the morning to fight traffic all day long, and assumed that every large attraction in the Park would have a campground nearby. Well, I paid for those mistakes.

To begin with, the forty miles from the south entrance to Old Faithful is a real bear of a climb, especially if taken as the second half of a day's ride, and done while traffic is heavy. The stretch is one of the busiest in the Park, and crosses the Continental Divide *three* times. I had no knowledge of the narrow roads, of how motorists will slam on brakes at the first sight of elk or buffalo, of the fact that the Old Faithful area does *not* have a campground, and that reservations for the Inn should be made far in advance. So let me now suggest a much more pleasant ride. I'll provide the route, distances, and information on services, and *you* worry about doing your miles early (if you're here at peak tourist times), and getting to the campgrounds before they're filled.

Begin the Yellowstone tour at the **South Entrance** (where you should pick up a map of the park if you don't already have one), and pedal north for twenty-two miles to **West Thumb**. (The park map will indicate that you've passed Lewis Falls and Grant Village—both of which have campgrounds. Continue to consult the map for services, and, when determining the length of your daily rides, assume you'll be making many stops *between* the major sites as well.) Don't turn left at West Thumb; instead, pedal north along beautiful Yellowstone Lake for twenty-one miles to **Fishing Bridge.** From here, go north again for sixteen miles to **Canyon**, and take time for the magnificent falls of the Yellowstone River. Then head north once more for nineteen miles to **Tower-Roosevelt,** and west for eighteen more to one of the prettiest areas of all—**Mammoth Hot Springs.** Here, multi-colored limestone terraces sit shimmering in steam, as boiling waters pour from one rock level to the next. Beyond the formation is a lovely green valley, stretching toward the mountains of Montana.

Turn south from Mammoth for the twenty-one-mile ride past Obsidian Cliff and Grizzly Lake to **Norris**—home of Geyser Basin. It's fourteen miles southwest from there to **Madison**, and then only sixteen more due south to **Old Faithful**. Because of all there is to see in that last stretch, I strongly suggest you try to spend the night in the grand Old Faithful Inn. Paint pots, geysers, waterfalls, and lovely hikes require that you spend some time in the area. But if this isn't possible you can camp at Madison, and pedal down and back a couple of times. And finally, it's only fourteen miles more from Madison to **West Yellowstone, Montana.** (If you aren't pedalling home you can rent a car in West Yellowstone, or grab a bus or plane there. If you are riding home, and wish to leave from the South Entrance, just plan to pedal the Old Faithful–West Thumb stretch very early in the morning.)

Of course, there are alternative routes (and even means) of travel in the Park. If you haven't time to do the entire north loop, head west from Canyon to Norris, and shave off forty-six miles (the entire loop—from West Thumb and back—is 125 miles). Or if you'd like to leave the bike for a while, air-conditioned buses travel to and from almost all areas of Yellowstone.

Ride carefully, suspend all food high above the ground at night, and have a *grand* time.